Don Megson
A Life in Football

Don Megson
A Life in Football

Don Megson with Chris Olewicz

VERTICAL EDITIONS
www.verticaleditions.com

First published in the United Kingdom in 2014 by Vertical Editions, Unit 4a, Snaygill Industrial Estate, Skipton, North Yorkshire BD23 2QR

www.verticaleditions.com

ISBN 978-1-904091-89-9

A CIP catalogue record for this book is available from the British Library

Cover design by HBA, York

Printed and bound by CMP (uk) Ltd, Poole, Dorset

For Yvonne and Patricia

Contents

Acknowledgements 9

Prologue: June 20th, 2011 11

1 The Jet Set 13

2 Roebuck 23

3 PTI 33

4 Losing End 44

5 Hobos 60

6 Darlings of the West End...75

7 Chasing Shadows 84

8 The Road to Wembley..93

9 Walking on Broadway 102

10 Singing Cushie Butterfield 113

11 Gas Head 124

12 Medals in My Eyes 132

13 Treading Water...145

14 City of Roses 156

15 Lock Out 166

16 Signing a Superstar 176

17 Blowing Smoke...185

Epilogue: A Life in Football...194

Acknowledgements

Don Megson

Chris first suggested the possibility of collaborating on a book of my career in football after an interview for his previous book. I'd been asked a number of times over the years if I was going to tell my story, and I thought that the timing was now right. I hope you enjoy the book. I have been blessed in life, and I'd like to thank my family, and all the players I played with and managed for making it possible.

Don Megson
Sheffield, October 2014

Chris Olewicz

As a witness to so many great footballing moments, Don Megson has approached the writing of this book with verve and gusto, and enriched it with his memories and his unique style. I would like to thank him for the patience he showed throughout the many hours of interviews that make this book as good as it can be. Football biographies are so numerous that it can be hard to tell, but Don has put his all into retelling the story of his life in football.

Tom Whitworth inspired me to take on the project and offered advice when I badly needed it. Jack Mansell's recollections of coaching Don as a player enrich and inform the narrative. The staff at the Sheffield Local History Archives were extremely forgiving in my efforts to examine their entire collection of newspaper clippings. Keith Farnsworth was as authoritative as ever in his recollections of Sheffield Wednesday in the 1960s. His books are a benchmark for all Wednesday fans.

Peter Warner and John Bain were generous in their reminiscences of Don's time at Portland Timbers, as was Michael Orr, whose knowledge of the Timbers was extensive. The San Diego Chicken Man provided vital corroboration. Mike Jay and Ian Haddrell, Bristol Rovers historians, were equally important reference points for this non Gas Head. Keith Brookman of Bristol Rovers and Neil Vacher of Bournemouth were both helpful in retrieving photographs of Don from his time in management.

My family were there to support me and to query me at regular interviews as to when the book was going to see the light of day. As was Keshia, who provided important support as the book neared completion. To them, and all others who read this book, I hope you enjoy reading about Don's journey. It is a story that for fans of Sheffield Wednesday and Bristol, needed telling, for it reminds us that in spite of ups and downs, the joy of football can never be extinguished.

Chris Olewicz
Sheffield, October 2014

Prologue

June 20th, 2011

In late June 2011, I headed to the Look Local Stadium in Stocksbridge to watch a Sheffield Wednesday XI play against Stocksbridge Park Steels. My son Gary had been manager of Wednesday since February of that year and spirits were high. Signings made the previous winter had settled, and the team looked odds on for automatic promotion in the coming season. Gary was optimistic.

At half time, in between discussions with Gary lamenting a poor performance from the youngsters, I got talking to a man who recognised me as Don Megson, ex-Wednesday player. He asked me when was the last time I'd visited the ground. I told him it had been at least fifty years way back at the start of my playing career, but I still recognised it as it hadn't changed a bit.

When I was just starting out, my dad often drove me to Sheffield from Manchester to play for Wednesday's Hatchard League team. We'd chug across the Pennines until we reached Hillsborough, where a coach would be waiting to take me on to wherever the team was playing. One weekend, we arrived to find that the coach to Stocksbridge had already set off. Johnny Logan, one of the coaches, was still at the ground and he asked my dad if he'd be able to fit a skip of shirts and balls into the back of his car. My dad reassured him that they would fit in no problem.

The skip turned out to be a huge wicker basket. We struggled to get it in the boot which refused to close properly, and set off for Stocksbridge, built on one side of a valley, with steel works on the other. Neither my dad nor I knew that the stadium was located half way up the hill. The car made a valiant effort to get up there, but with all the weight the engine gave out. We had to ditch, and push it the rest of the way up, with the skip bulging out. I can't remember anything about the car, but I'll never forget pushing it up that hill.

One of the hobbies I took up when I retired from football was golf. I've always enjoyed playing four ball with my friends Carl Booth, and Ken and Garry Biggins. We have competitive games, good laughs, and always have time for an enjoyable pint when we're in the clubhouse. Carl and Gary are staunch Sheffield United fans, and Ken and I represent Sheffield Wednesday, so there's always a lot of banter when I'm asked to recount one of the stories from my career. More often than not, the conversation will turn to the 1966 FA Cup Final and how Wednesday lost their 2-0 lead against Everton.

Of course, that was the big game, the biggest of my career. But it was just one day – one game – of a career that took in hundreds of games. After that many, details can become fuzzy, but what stays with you are the moments of camaraderie, sportsmanship, and family. I was at Sheffield Wednesday for seventeen years as a player. After that I played for and then managed Bristol Rovers for seven years to some success before I left for the United States to manage Portland Timbers in the North American Soccer League. After that came an unforgettable six months at Bournemouth over the summer of 1983.

All those experiences took place in the context of building a loving family with my wife Yvonne. At a time when footballers weren't paid the world and didn't expect it, everything that I did went towards building a future for her and my sons, Gary and Neil. Without them, my life would have been a poorer place. I dedicate this book to them.

As we reach the seventh hole, I hear the inevitable question. 'Don, what did it feel like to lose the FA Cup Final?'

'You know what lads,' I reply, 'how about this for a story?'

1

The Jet Set

In the late summer of 1959 Eric Taylor, General Manager of Sheffield Wednesday Football Club, called me to his office at Hillsborough Stadium to discuss my future in football. There was a lot to talk about. I was twenty-three years old and had been at the club for seven years. I'd played over a hundred games in the amateur and reserve leagues, had just completed my National Service, and was at the point where I had to decide what I was going to do for a living.

I could hardly call my footballing career up to that point a success. Numerous players had been promoted ahead of me into the Wednesday first team while I'd worked as a joiners apprentice in my home city of Manchester. Week in, week out, I'd wait for a telegram to fall through my letter box, alerting me to the fact that I was expected at Hillsborough the following weekend to play in a game. There'd be no indication of where I'd be going, who I'd be playing against, or in what position I'd be playing.

On the morning, I'd catch a bus from Sale to Manchester, passing by the industrial estates, and get on a train to Sheffield at Piccadilly Station. Once in Sheffield, I'd board the tram to Hillsborough where I'd either prepare for a home game at Owlerton Stadium or board a coach headed for Ossett or Kiveton or wherever we happened to be playing that afternoon. I'd catch up with the other players, play the game, pick up my £2.50 match fee, and then repeat the same journey home. It was a stretch.

I've yet to find out why the club persisted in involving me for so many years without a hint as to whether I was going to get near the first team. Eric, who'd been manager for nearly all of my time there, was a suit and tie man. I don't think he ever led a coaching session or put on a track suit in his life. That's not to say that he didn't know football, as he spent many an evening scouting players and was steeped in the game. But I don't think he ever watched me play so as to form an opinion of whether I was worth a run in the first team. He left that to the coaching staff.

In the time I'd spent doing my National Service, Eric had decided to relinquish control of the first team to a dedicated team manager and concentrate on his administrative duties. For the first time since the war the manager position was vacant. A number of names were suggested by the media, including Bill Nicholson of Tottenham, but in the end the board hired Harry Catterick, who'd made his managerial career on shoestring budgets at Crewe and Rochdale. I'd yet to meet him, but Wednesday had won the Second Division in his first season so it seemed like the right decision.

The offices of Hillsborough were focused around a central room with benches placed around a billiard table. When visiting Hillsborough on business, that room was where you reported. It is now part of the changing rooms. On this particular day everything was quiet while at other times it was a hive of activity. I'd seen Jackie Sewell and the media circus bustling through on the day Jackie had signed in 1953. This was a club that mattered, and I was rubbing shoulders.

'Mr Taylor will see you now.'

As I walked into Eric's office, I felt uneasy, not really knowing what was happening. A trip to Eric's office meant that something important was going to be discussed. I sat down on the near side of his half-moon shaped desk. 'How is your family Don?' he asked me. 'Are you keeping well?' Then he offered a full time professional contract. 'Things are moving fast.' I said.

That much was true. I'd gone into National Service promising to get married to my girlfriend Yvonne on completion, but plans changed. I left the army a husband and a father. Now all of those uncertainties appeared a little more distant to me. Here was a chance of full time football. Thoughts of a daily commute from Manchester and a chance at the first team crossed my mind, so I accepted immediately.

*****

Two weeks later I was back in Hillsborough to meet Harry. He was an intimidating presence and took his work very seriously; His office had papers scattered all around it, the sign of a frantic mind. He told me that he wanted to bring down the age of the first team and was willing to try players in different positions to see if their strengths could be better utilised. Though he left most of the training to Tommy Eggleston he'd seen me train as a centre half, and told me that my chances of getting into the first team were slim. 'I've got three centre halves Don, so I want you to try out at left full back.'

On reflection, if I'd moved to left back sooner, Hugh Swift, or another coach, might have mentioned to Eric Taylor that I was doing okay in that position and that might have warranted me a chance in the first team a lot earlier. I might even have got in there as a part-timer. Hugh and Johnny got the feeling that I'd be in the first team by Christmas and I started to feel the same way.

I began commuting from Manchester on the 8.00am train to Sheffield and I'd meet up with the other players who lived locally. Joining me in our regular compartment would be Don Gibson, George Kirby and Johnny Ballagher. Further on, we'd pick up the twins Derek and Eric Wilkinson in Aston. I knew them all from the A League, where I'd played the majority of my matches for Wednesday.

After just fifteen matches in the reserves I made my début for the first team against Burnley on November 14th, 1959. Peter Johnson, the right full back, got injured and Norman Curtis, the left back, moved over to the right to fill in. Norman, nicknamed 'Cannonball' due to his penalty kick prowess, was in his mid-thirties and winding down. I remember walking to Owlerton with him at the start of the season. He was scanning a copy of the fixture list, 'Another seventeen games to go and I might get a game against Stan Matthews,' he told me. I thought to myself, no you won't because I am playing in your position.

The team sheets were usually posted after Friday training. It was then that you found out where you'd be going, or nowhere as the case might have been. I felt a little sorry for Norman because he never got back in the first team and was sold to Doncaster Rovers soon after. But that's just how football is. He'd have been hoping that I wouldn't make so much of an impression as to become an automatic first choice. Jack Martin had been filling in for Peter that season, so it was unfortunate for him as well.

Back home in Manchester, it was celebration time at my wife Yvonne's parents house. During the party, there was a knock on the door. The Manchester Evening Gazette had got wind of the news and wanted to take a photograph of me, Yvonne and Gary. It was the first picture taken of me as a professional footballer.

On the Saturday, the ritual was the same – bus to Piccadilly then train to Sheffield. It was only when I got in the home dressing room that I realised that this was something different. When I heard the roar of the crowd coming from the top of the tunnel, I felt a rush of energy that I'd feel hundreds of times more. Tommy Eggleston's last words to me were, 'If it stands above two foot and it's got a different coloured shirt on, tackle it as hard as you can.'

Burnley weren't too dissimilar to us as a club, except that instead of building up their stadium, they'd invested heavily in their training centre. The investment had worked as only one of their forwards that day had cost a fee. Jimmy Robson had come from the youth team, John Connelly, the England right winger had signed from St Helens, and Brian Pilkington, who also played for England, had come from Leyland Motors.

As a left back, my main role was to keep the outside right quiet, and to tackle him hard if he was causing me too much trouble. If I could do that, then I could say I'd done well. It wasn't a particularly memorable game, a 1-1 draw, and it wasn't easy marking John Connelly. I was partly responsible for the goal scored against us. Tom McAnearney and Jimmy McIlroy were tussling with the ball right near our by-line, waiting for each other to make the first move. Tom of course, was happy to count down the seconds for the whistle.

All of a sudden, Tony Kay came running in behind and scythed through Jimmy who went crashing down. The referee gave a free kick and I was put in to cover the far post. Brian Pilkington swept a ball in at head height and Peter Swan looked as though he was going to head it away but missed it. It hit me on the chest and set up Jimmy Robson who pushed it into the net.

In the dressing room after the game, Tom gave Tony an earful, about how he'd acted immaturely and robbed us of the win. Tony just smirked and made jokes about 'Old Man' McAnearney. We all laughed. It was quite an introduction.

My entry into the team coincided with the start of an extended unbeaten run. We only lost four more games that season and came close to winning the title. We played some exquisite football in the run up to Christmas. The next week we beat Leeds at Elland Road, with Bobby Craig, a new signing from Third Lanark, making his début. Harry had been tracking him for nearly six months which is a long time to wait to spend £7,000.

Over Christmas we beat West Ham 7-0, Chelsea 4-0 and Arsenal 5-1, which made our Christmas party at the Royal Oak a real occasion. On the train back to Manchester, Don Gibson suggested that we carry on the party at the famous Cabaret Club. We arrived, settled into a booth, and ordered some champagne. As we drank, the Kray twins walked through the bar and went through a door into one of the back rooms. We heard that they were in the area on business with the Manchester gangs.

Don then suggested it would be fun to go out to Fallowfield to visit Matt Busby. He was married to his daughter Sheena. Matt had a very gentle and welcoming nature, and though you imagined him to be a little aggrieved at strangers turning up unannounced, he didn't let it show. From that day on he became a lifelong friend, and I never received any less than a good reception whenever I needed anything from him.

*****

Our good run extended into the FA Cup. In the third round we played Middlesbrough who were a big physical side. Their line-up contained winger Eddie Holliday and Brian Clough, both of whom had recently broken into the England team. We beat them though, and I remember thinking that we were really starting to show how solid we'd made the defence.

We beat Peterborough in the fourth round in a tough match won with a bit of luck, to face Manchester United at Old Trafford. Though I'd played at Old Trafford for the reserves, this time it was for real. Lining up against us was Albert Quixall, Dennis Viollett, Bobby Charlton, Maurice Setters and Harry Gregg. The night before the match, Albert and Dennis had made some cocky remarks to the Manchester newspapers saying that the match would be a pushover. It revved us up and made us more eager to beat them.

I was ecstatic to be playing and put in a match-winning performance marking Warren Bradley. Every tackle seemed to come off right for me. We almost went behind after a chance from Albert, but Peter Swan managed to get back and clear the ball off the line. His clearance was picked up by John Fantham who raced into the box and won a penalty off Maurice Setters. Tom McAnearney stepped up, and burst the net to make it 1-0, which is how it stayed.

Because I was a local lad, the press asked me before the kick-off if I'd like to do an interview after the game. As soon as the final whistle blew, I was whisked away by the media with Albert Quixall, who'd left Wednesday the previous season. We jumped in a car and were driven up a side street to a derelict old church. We went inside, the crew set up, and then we were shoved in front of the camera. 'So Don, what did you think about the game?' I could hardly get the words out, I was that excited about having won the match.

The quarter-final draw gave us Sheffield United at Bramall Lane. We were pummelled, but somehow managed to come away with a win. Derek Wilkinson, who'd not been in the greatest form that season, had asked Harry if he could be dropped from the first team but Harry responded by telling him to play himself out of his bad spell. Though we had the better players, we were only in the game for about fifteen minutes, but in that time, Derek managed to get two goals. Keith Ellis was involved in both, getting up past Joe Shaw to flick the ball on for the first, and then dummying a ball from Bobby Craig for the second. I imagine that Harry hadn't meant that much by his off-the-cuff remark, but it worked wonders for Derek.

We were the better team against Blackburn in the semi-final, and all the newspapers expected us to win and get through to the final, but sadly we fell at the last hurdle. We let in a goal from Derek Dougan early on that should never have been allowed. He was as far offside as it was possible to be. Then it got worse. Derek Wilkinson got the ball out on the wing, ran down with it, and then knocked it over to Alan Finney who shot into the net. The referee gave the goal, but then changed his mind and gave Derek offside. I'm convinced that if we'd have got that goal we would have gone on to win the game.

That defeat really took the wind out of us. We won the next match at Hillsborough against Manchester United, but only managed to win two games from our last eight to finish fifth, six points off Burnley. I didn't think much of it at the time, but we really missed out that season. The league was really tight and Burnley only managed to win it on the final day, having not previously occupied the top spot. People forget how close we were.

*****

The end of the season brought a few weeks rest before we set off to the Soviet Union on tour. We'd played a friendly against one of the Soviet sides earlier that season, and as a reward, we'd been chosen to be the UK representative on the return trip. It was my first trip abroad, and I quickly learned that tours were as much about team building as playing football.

Being local, Derek Wilkinson and I arranged to meet up with the rest of the players at Manchester Airport. The day before, I went to visit my childhood barber Mr White, which later became a tradition whenever I went back home to visit my parents. I walked in and sat in the chair, not thinking that he'd not seen me in years. The razor was turned on and immediately I felt the 'buzz' go right up the back of my head for short back and sides. It was too late, I was stuck with it.

The next day I caught the bus to Manchester Airport to meet up with Derek and the rest of the team. He didn't even look at my head, let alone mention the haircut, and half an hour went by before the team coach pulled up. Derek jumped up, sprinted over to the coach and clambered the steps. I saw him talking and one by one the players came to the window, pointing at their heads with big grins on their faces. For the entirety of the tour I was called 'The Mohican.'

We flew on the de Havilland Comet to Switzerland, and then on to Moscow. The hotel was a magnificent old building, big and immaculate, complete with a big hammer and sickle above the entrance. After dinner, Tommy Eggleston, who thought the food wasn't on the ball, asked for eggs to be served at breakfast. When we came down the stairs the next morning, we found a big bowl of uncooked eggs parked in the middle of the table. Tommy flew into the kitchen to find out what he could do with them but I don't think he had much luck.

As part of the welcome, we were invited to the British Embassy for a lunchtime reception. I expected a relaxed affair, chit-chatting politics over a few gin and tonics. We arrived at the building, and made our way onto the lawn, but about ten minutes later Eric sidled over to our group and told us quietly, 'Make your way to the gate please. Make your way to the exit.' Once we were assembled outside, we were told that we'd arrived at the wrong party. To the guests, we were just a group of gate crashers who'd walked in off the street.

After that mishap, we went to see the Red Square. Keith Gardiner, one of the board members, decided that we should visit the pavilion in the Central Park of Culture and Rest, where the captured U2 spy plane was displayed. Then we went around the corner to see Lenin and Stalin in the Mausoleum. The queue was miles long, but thanks to our 'celebrity' status we were filed through to the front. Afterwards, I bought myself a Russian hat which was about the only item on sale in the gift shops.

The first match was arranged for the same afternoon as a May Day parade, and we were the warm up act. We lost 1-0 against CSKA Moscow with Lev Yashin, the famous goalkeeper, guesting. During the match I was injured when the outside right sat on my knee. It was my first notable injury, and both Tony Kay and I were unable to play in the next match in Tbilisi, Georgia.

Tbilisi was a provincial city, and an eye opener culture wise with statues of Stalin everywhere. Everyone was dressed the same, and all the men sported thick Sam Costa-style moustaches. We were followed everywhere by the KGB. The day before the match we travelled up to a restaurant in the hills outside the city that was accessible only by cable car.

On the day of the match, news reached the city of the Turkish Revolt, a military coup d'état. There were loudspeakers everywhere blurting out the comments of Russian leaders on the situation, but none of the locals on the streets were taking any notice. As we walked along we were harassed by people shouting impassioned pleas for 'Billets!' We lost the game.

We returned to Moscow with injuries galore. We had heard that a Swedish team were also touring the area and Eric got in contact with their Embassy to see if there were any wing-halves that we could borrow. Unfortunately, they had moved on out of the country. Then he appealed to the Soviet F.A. for some ringers, but the authorities told him that Muscovites would not take kindly to the appearance of a Russian in a foreign team.

Harry and Tom were already anxious when on the day before the game against Lokomotiv, Derek Wilkinson joined them in the lift at the hotel. 'Bad news boss,' he said. 'I've got a septic toe.' Fortunately, Derek was able to play in the end, and Tony and I managed to hobble through the match.

The day before we were due to fly home we were invited to visit a ski jump, a traditional pastime for Muscovites in the winter. At this time of year however, there was no snow, but we were invited up to the top to admire the view. Once there, James Gunstone, another director who always came with us on the tours, decided to look over the edge. His false teeth came out and fell all the way down to ground level.

A great time was had by all. Harry got really close to the players on tours and would come out of his shell. It was nice to see another side of him. He enjoyed a drink and would always go a little over the top. On the last night, he poured a drink in Peter Johnson's newly purchased balalaika.

Then the flight home, and the long wait for the start of the next season.

2

Roebuck

I was born Donald Harry Megson on June 12th, 1936 in Sale, which enjoyed a good reputation at the time. It was home to several Manchester United footballers and unlike other areas, wasn't dominated by a single industry. There were people from all walks of life. I was brought up in a terraced house on Washway Road, which in history had been Watling Street, the main Roman road from Chester to London. There were about twenty terraced houses on our stretch, with an off license on one end and a plumber on the other. The previous occupants of our house had turned the front room into a shop, and my parents had decided to take it on when they'd moved in. Our living area was in the back, with the bedrooms upstairs.

It certainly wasn't poverty. Every morning we'd mark up the newspapers for delivery, light the fire range, and turn on the radio that was powered by a car battery. But there were limitations. There was no central heating, so every night there were long discussions over who was going to have the oven shelf in their bed. There was a tin bath that used to hang up on the wall outside in the yard, and it was my job to tip out the jerry bowl for the outside toilet, which was horrendous. Toys were scarce and my first real toy was a battered old rocking horse that my brothers Derek, Cyril and I rode until it fell to pieces.

When World War II broke out my father David joined the army as a dispatch rider, so it was mum who brought us up. Dad would visit from time to time during the fighting, rifle in hand, but I didn't really know him. He received the South Africa Star for his services in the North Africa Campaign and fought in the Battle of Monte Casino. Hearing those stories for the first time in my life, and then hearing them again when I was fifty, delivered with the same passion, I knew that it was probably the highlight of his life, a moment when things really mattered.

My childhood experiences were those of a typical war baby. While the adults struggled with being bombed and separated from loved ones, my war was the excitement of search lights and barrage balloons. Getting up in the middle of the night to go and play in the air raid shelter, listening to the sirens as they got progressively louder as a raid began. Afterwards, we'd go out into the garden and watch Manchester centre lit up by the fires that the bombs had caused.

I had stacks of friends. My next door neighbour was Dennis Young, an ARP assistant, and Fred Wadsworth, who lived just across the road. Then there were school friends like Jim MacMillan, Tony Logan, Bob Lamb, Nev Miller, and the brothers Joe and Brian Curran. Nearly every night after we'd finished tea, we'd congregate on Roebuck Field, which separated Roebuck from the Wythenshawe overspill estate.

We'd all been left with memories of German bombings and dogfights over our houses, and the games we played always reflected this. One game we used to play was parachutes. This was sheets tied together with string and weighted with rocks before being thrown off the roof of an Anderson shelter. This got more ambitious, until one day, Nev decided that it would be a good idea to make a homemade hand grenade using Carbide, which at the time was used as a form of lighting for cars and cycles.

Nev bought the carbide from Barnes Cycle Shop, and a trial run was set up in his Aunt Minnie's back garden which already looked a bit like a battlefield having been dug over for vegetables in the war. He mixed the Carbide with water in a glass bottle which created loads of smoke and gas. He threw the bottle and then ducked below the vegetables for safety.

Unfortunately, the bottle didn't explode, not until Nev decided to try and pick it up. It exploded in his hand and damaged his eye. The doctor was called, and he was taken to Manchester Royal Eye Hospital, where it was removed. Nev spent six weeks recovering, and missed his 11-plus examination that summer. He took it later that year, and out of all of us, he was the only one to go to grammar school.

In all the years I've known Nev, he's never felt sorry for himself or moaned about having bad luck. He's overcome any problems head on, and worked to become head manager of a well known insurance firm. I never heard anyone have a bad word to say about him, and I've always had a high regard for him because of the way that he faced his situation. He later emigrated to Australia with his wife Pauline and son Brad.

As we grew older the games changed. Parachutes turned into kiss chase with the 'Roebuck Lads' chasing the 'Wythenshawe Girls.' Inevitably, we started pairing off into couples doing our own thing, visiting each other's houses. I first met Yvonne at a dance at the Locarno. I'd played for Manchester Youth by that time, and I used to wear their badge on my blazer. As I walked into the room, Yvonne leaned over to her friend Mavis Langhorn and said, 'I'm going to marry him.'

Once we'd started courting, Nev got upset that I wasn't spending any time with the lads. 'You're going soft on her Don. Better get rid of her and get back to the lads.' Stupidly, but predictably, I took his advice seriously, and told Yvonne that we were through. Nev went and asked her out!

*****

I was nine when dad came home. It was intimidating at first because I'd never had a man around the house. As far as I knew, mum was in charge, and all of a sudden that changed. Suddenly, I started hearing 'You wait until your father gets home.' Of course, he fought like hell to get to know me, and spent as much time with me as possible.

Sport had always been a big part of my family. Dad had actually played at outside right for Manchester City, and never ceased to tell me about it, even though it must have only been half a dozen games. Both he and his brother Arthur were athletes, and he was also a good sprinter, cricketer and snooker player.

Being so close to Old Trafford, I naturally became a Manchester United fan, and dad decided to take me to Old Trafford with my friend Dennis Young. I can remember thinking that it was impossible that Joe Mercer was able to play football seeing how bow-legged he was. Then the magic happened, and he passed the ball to Johnny Carey who knocked a shot just over the bar. As he turned round, he caught sight of me at the front of the crowd and winked. I was hooked.

1948 was a big year for United as they won the FA Cup against Blackpool. Even now I can rattle off the team. I went to Princes Parkway to watch them bring the Cup home. The players were on the bus, including my heroes Jack Rowley and Johnny Carey, and I thought, I want to do that one day.

That summer, the Australian Cricket team arrived to compete for the Ashes, and I fell in love with the image of the Australian cricket cap. Don Bradman was the star, and it became my whole world to try and watch him in the flesh. We couldn't get to Leeds to watch the Test Match however, so my dad took me to Old Trafford instead to watch Lancashire play Yorkshire. Playing that day was Jack Ikin and Cyril Washbrook for Lancashire, and Johnny Wardle for Yorkshire.

Academically speaking I was an absolute nightmare, and never really got on with the classes at school. Eventually, the teachers sort of cast me to one side in the classes and focused on those that could handle the English and the maths. It later transpired that I was dyslexic, but of course that wasn't a factor back then.

But when it came to sports I excelled. It was Mr Sharp, the gym teacher, who got me into the Poplar Grove football team and made me captain. On one occasion Jack Rowley came to do a coaching session and we had all been told to call him Sir. But with him being my idol, I couldn't help myself and when shouting for the ball, I yelled 'Jack' 'Jack.' Sharp called me over: 'Megson. It's Sir. You call him Sir. I rushed back into the game and instantly forgot what he'd just told me. 'Jack.'

fifteen years later, when I was playing for Wednesday, we travelled to Amsterdam to play Ajax. I didn't know it but Jack was their manager at the time. As Wednesday's coach pulled up to the front of the stadium, I looked out of the window and saw him walking past. My mind flew back to 1948. It was the same for me with the excitement and enthusiasm that kids were giving me outside Hillsborough.

Football wasn't the only sport I played. An early achievement was throwing javelin for Cheshire at the All England Sports Finals. A well spoken music teacher had spotted my enthusiasm and asked me if I wanted to learn how to throw. 'Not half,' I replied. So he marked me out a track, and taught me how to do the steps. 'OK Donald,' he shouted. 'Off you go.' I practised for hours and hours and soon enough became pretty good at it.

When it was time for the Finals in Southampton I did well on my first throw, and was in second place after the second. All of a sudden someone came up to me and told me I was needed down at the athletics track as a member of the relay team had gone AWOL and I had to fill in. I ran the two miles to the track to do the second leg of the relay race but of course we didn't win. I like to win, so deciding to run meant that I thought I had a chance. England Sports was a good standard. After the race, I ran straight back to throw my third javelin. Given the circumstances, it wasn't a surprise that I didn't improve on second position.

I also tried my hand at cricket. My brother Cyril used to work for Lino-Type, who made printing presses, and he played for their cricket team, as well as the football team. One day, he told me that the team was short of players, and asked whether I'd like to go and play. I'd bowled for the school team, and knew the distances for delivering. So I borrowed some whites, and took a few wickets, and a great catch off Cyril's bowling. It was an absolute bullet that stuck to my hands. Cyril was talking me up, 'Ey' he's no mug. He's not bad is he!'

Then I go into bat. We needed two more runs to win, but only had one over left to get them. Facing me was a spin bowler and I was determined not to get out. The first ball was pitched in and I played it square, nice and steady. Then I did it again. I only went

27

and blocked all six shots. The fact that we needed the points had gone completely out of my mind.

I walked off the pitch proud as punch. I'd survived the shots. As I approached the pavilion, Cyril marched up to me, 'What the hell were you doing? We only needed two. Why didn't you have a swing? We could have won the bloody game.' Back in the pavilion eating my cucumber sandwiches I felt about one inch tall. I definitely marked myself out as an individual that day. I'd been more concerned with not getting out than getting the points we needed.

Cyril was a better football prospect than I ever was. He was a fantastic dribbler and could take people on and leave them behind. He had trials for Burnley and Manchester City, and had a reasonable time playing for Altrincham, Hyde and Stalybridge. But he was more interested in girls than football and he'd always be on his bike riding to his girlfriend's house. He came home one day with the record of Peg O' My Heart by Joe Loss and played it repeatedly. I remember telling him, 'What are you doing mooning about with a girl with all your talent?'

My other brother Derek was nine years older than me, so I wasn't as close to him. When he was seventeen he developed a bone disease in his thigh – I remember the day that the ambulance came and carried him away on a stretcher to have his leg drained. He never got involved in sport, but did take up body building, and finished with a good physique. He used to bring Charles Atlas books home with him, and had a picture of him carrying the world on his shoulder on the wall.

It was Cyril who set me on course for Wednesday. In 1951, he signed from Lino-Type's football team to Mossley, where he played as an outside right for seven years. To begin with he was under a manager named Jack Boothway. I came home from work one day, and was getting ready to go out, when my dad told Cyril: 'Why don't you take Don with you?'

'I can't do that Dad,' Cyril replied as he left the house.

A few weeks later, Cyril told me he'd spoken to Jack, and that I could go along to Mossley with him the next week. On the day, we caught the 47 bus into Manchester, and boarded a white minibus that was laid on for all the Manchester lads who played for Mossley. There were about eight of us, and it was a real education hearing the talk, the swearing and the banter. From that day on, the banter was a part of my life, and I wanted to be a footballer more than ever.

The Cheshire League was a good standard at that time, and Seel Park, the Mossley ground, was a smart little thing. I started pre-season training with Cyril playing in five-a-sides. Though I was still only fifteen I was a pretty decent size and was beginning to feel more comfortable playing against fully grown men. I was still playing for Poplar Grove when one day Cyril came home, 'Don!' he shouted, 'I've had a row with Jack. He said to me 'Don will never make a player as long as he's got a hole in his arse, so next time you go to training, show him what you can do.'

Up to that point I'd been treating the Mossley training as a little bit of fun, but the next time I went I decided not to act like a wallflower. I started to put myself about a bit, going in for tackles and whacking a few players. At that time, I had in my mind that a good player was someone who handled the ball well and knocked killer passes. But I quickly settled for playing to my strengths, being a good defensive reader of the game, and stopping the players who could play.

I always put as much effort in as I could to improve. I used to spend a lot of time in the back yard, coaching myself through practice. I'd see a chip in my mind's eye, and would try to copy it in real time. Jimmy Delaney, a flag pole, would be on the right wing, and Jack Rowley, a dustbin, would be in the middle. On the other side of the yard was Charlie Mitten at outside left. He was a gate. I'd kick a ball against the flag pole and that would tell me that I'd hit a successful pass to Jimmy Delaney. Then I'd hit it up to the dustbin and if I missed, I'd know I'd missed Jack Rowley.

The fences around the back were about six feet high, so I could play wall passes wherever I liked. I used to practice for hours to get the touch to bring a ball down dead. One day I put in a brilliant shot that clipped the top of a coping stone and went straight through next door's window. I walked into the house, and though mum wasn't angry, she told me I'd have to pay for it myself. Cyril, who couldn't keep a straight face, asked, 'Was it in?'

'No, it clipped the top of the bar.'

'Oh, well. Try and keep it down next time.'

*****

Not long after I started training regularly for Mossley, Jack picked me to play against Buxton. I only played one other match, against Winsford, before a scout from Manchester Youth spoke to Jock Anderson, who was one of the trainers. He told Jock that he had a good outside left there, then asked if he could also play outside right.

'He can play anywhere,' Jock replied. 'In defence, midfield and up front.' I hadn't even played in those positions before but I was picked to represent Manchester Youth at Crewe as an outside right. From there it snowballed. During the warm down I was approached by a man called Ted Schofield and my eyes lit up. I thought I was about to be scouted for Manchester United or Manchester City, but he said he was from Sheffield Wednesday.

He asked if I'd like to have a trial. I'd never played for England School Boys and didn't have much of a profile, so I knew that I'd done something to impress him. Later that same week he came over to my house and told me that he'd recommended me to Wednesday. I was to report at Hillsborough on the following Saturday. I signed amateur forms and was told how much I would be paid in expenses.

On the day, my dad rushed around with his milk and paper round, picked me up and then drove me to Sheffield. Then I was on the coach to play in a Hatchard League game at Pennistone Church. The Hatchard League consisted of several 'Works' teams from the local area, such as Dinnington and Kiveton Park. The game was a low key affair, with spectators numbering zero. The pitch was a community playing field with a tennis court at one end.

The two men in charge of the team were Ted Catlin and Joe Nibloe, who'd starred for Wednesday as the full back pairing in the 1935 FA Cup Final against West Brom. I was selected to play as an outside right, which wasn't a good move because my right leg was only good for standing on. After the match, Ted told me, 'You played well today, but I'll tell you something. You ain't no outside right. Come back next week, and we'll try you on the left.' So I went back the next week and played outside left. Then I played the next week after that.

*****

Football has always been a temporary assignment, even so more in the early 1950s, and my dad was still keen for me to get a real job. He set me up at Deans, a building firm owned by David Dean, a former rugby player for Sale Rugby club. Dad delivered their milk and must have got talking to someone because he came home one day and asked me if I wanted to be a joiner. 'You don't have overalls you know, they have an apron.'

I said yes, thinking that I'd be able to wear an apron with all the tools. Of course, you only got those when you graduated to full joiner status. I never got out of overalls, doing the odd jobs and making tea. But I owe a debt to my dad. I didn't give him any credit for it at the time but I realise now that it was him looking out for me.

Things had gone okay at Deans for the first year, and I'd been promoted to senior apprentice. But it came to a sticky end. One day, a new boy came in five minutes late for work. The charge hand, a bloke called Albert Scelhorn started getting on at him, shouting about how he would lose a days pay for being late. Being the gobby sort, I decided to interfere. 'That's a bit harsh that, losing a days pay just for five minutes. What's the matter with you?'

Albert told me to mind my own business. I didn't take kindly to that, so I picked up a mallet and hit him on the head. As a bound apprentice, my union told Deans that I couldn't be sacked but Deans protested, stating the offence was too serious for me to carry on. So the union found me another company where I could finish. I ended up going to Matthew Cowans. The owner was a mad Manchester United fan who'd taken on many United apprentices when they were fifteen and kept them until they signed as professional players at seventeen. One example was Geoff Bent. He was a utility player who sadly died at Munich. He only travelled that day because my good friend Wilf McGuiness had broken his leg.

Cowans were brilliant with me, and I wished I'd been there longer. At Deans, we'd just made window frames for buildings. At Cowans, we did proper joinery work and I was allowed to get involved. The first job that I went on was putting a window in a larder, and it was a disaster. First, I accidentally smashed the glass before it went in and had to pay for some more. Then I mixed the concrete incorrectly and the bricks all dropped in the middle. It was a steep learning curve.

A few jobs later, we were putting a new ground floor ceiling in an old fashioned pub. We took the roof down, and I started cutting new beams. I measured the first one correctly, and it fitted in perfectly. So I decided to measure the others up to the same length. I was eager to impress, and was working really quickly, so the sweat was dropping off me.

The other guys came in, and picked up the first beam. It slotted in like a glove. They slotted in the next one, and it came up a little short. The third one was even shorter, and only just made it across the room. Turns out that being an old pub, the far wall had bellied, making the room a little wider in the middle, and I'd not bothered to measure them to check. It took me a while to live it down. All the other workers used to shout out, 'Watch him. He doesn't know what he's doing.'

3

PTI

As far as Yvonne was concerned, my footballing career only took off when I met her. She quickly got used to the idea of me disappearing on Saturdays to play football, joining her and the rest of the group in the evening after I got back.

Things were going fine until she mentioned to her father that I played for Sheffield Wednesday. Her father was a driver for Sykes Coaches, which ran away game coaches for the Manchester teams, and a few weeks later he came back from London and confronted her. He'd taken some Man City fans down to London that weekend and while there had seen the line up for Wednesday, who were also playing in London that day. Not seeing my name in the first team line-up, he'd presumed that I'd been lying to her. 'That lad that you're with, he doesn't play for Wednesday,' he told her. 'I don't want you seeing him anymore.' It didn't enter into his mind that I was only seventeen and might not have been in the first team.

Once Yvonne and I were married, he and I got on great. He loved the Sheffield Wednesday ties I was given by the club, and because I used to get new ones all the time, for tours and smart dress, I used to give him my old ones. He'd wear them that much that they'd disintegrate, and when it was time for a new one, I'd take off mine and give it to him. He was really proud of me, and he got plenty of conversation starters out of the ties.

I started courting Yvonne when she was fifteen and I'd just finished school. She'd passed her 11-plus and gone to high school. From the moment we met she always used to say, 'Don't you talk to me like that. I'm brainier than you.' Before computers came out, she worked for an insurance company as a comptometer operator

Without ever saying anything, she had my fate in her hands. We'd always said that we'd get married once I'd finished in the service, but as soon as she found out that I'd get paid more if we were married, it was a given. We got married on August 31st, 1959. As I was getting ready to go to the church, I turned to Cyril and said, 'How on earth did I get here?'

*****

I wasn't with Wednesday long before I was promoted to their A Team who played in the Yorkshire League. Eric Taylor recognised that the commute, coupled with my apprenticeship, meant that I wasn't able to train at Hillsborough on a regular basis and rather than exclude me, he spoke to Manchester United manager Matt Busby. Together, they arranged for me to train with the United squad at their training complex known as The Cliff on the banks of the River Irwell in Broughton.

On my first visit to The Cliff I was introduced to chief coach Jimmy Murphy and first team coach Bert Whalley. The facilities were light years ahead of anything I'd seen up to that point. Both Jimmy and Bert would coach 'during the game.' Jimmy in one match and Bert in the other. They'd coach the players how to play in certain situations. One team might be on the defensive and Jimmy would shout out to Wilf McGuinness, 'Pull back Wilf.' Or Bert might shout out to Duncan Edwards, 'Move forward Duncan, get out there.'

I understood how difficult if must have been to avoid giving a running commentary of the game, and they were both masters of getting what they wanted from the players. Though I was never allowed to play with them, I picked up lots of useful information about my game. I also got to know the Busby family quite well. Sandy Busby, who never made it as a footballer, used to be around the place quite a lot. It was a real pleasure to be mixing with the team I'd supported as a boy. I came home with

Bobby Charlton every Tuesday and Wednesday on the bus. He would get off at Old Trafford where he, Duncan Edwards and Dave Pegg lived in club houses at the Stretford end.

Despite the fact that I was only a part timer, I was utterly committed to keeping myself match fit. If there was a reason I couldn't make it to The Cliff – there might have been bad weather or another engagement – I made sure I got my fitness training in. I'd often do my training and my courting all at once. I'd set out to Yvonne's house, jogging from one lamp post to the next, and then sprinting to the next one and so on. When I arrived, I'd have a bath and change my clothes. I'd come home on the bus. I knew for a fact that not everyone had the discipline to do something like that but I had a deep desire to make it.

The A Team was a better standard than the Hatchard League. I met young players like Jim and Tom McAnearney, Keith Ellis and Peter Swan, who became my best friend at the club. The team was run by former Wednesday players John Logan and Hugh Swift, veterans of the late 1940s. Hugh had been a first team regular, and had played for the England 'B' side. In football, certain types of players register with certain styles of coaching, and his candour resonated with me.

Home matches were played on a pitch to the rear of Owlerton Stadium, not far from Hillsborough. At one time, they'd played on the grass in the middle of the dog track, but it wasn't giving the players the correct perspective of what a match environment was like as it was too small, so we moved to another pitch at the rear of the stadium. After the game, we'd wash and change, and run down Penistone Road to Hillsborough as fast as we could to watch the first team. We'd make our way into the player's pen and watch Derek Dooley star for the first team. At the time he was in the middle of his great scoring streak, and seeing him in full flight with his shirt flapping everywhere, going through a brick wall to score, was exhilarating.

The Hatchard League had been a place for trialists more than anything, but the A Team were almost all full-time professionals, and players who'd experienced first team football, mixed in with part time professionals and apprentices. I was in there as a part-time professional, so I could continue with my apprenticeship, as were Colin Dobson and Gerry Young. Jack Shaw was one of those players who had come down from the first team to wind down his career. He was a father figure to a lot of the youngsters, and taught us a lot about how to look after ourselves on the pitch.

Tackling in those days was a lot tastier, and you had to learn how to handle yourself. An example was when I was playing centre half at Rawmarsh Welfare. In the opposition team was a striker who'd played for Rotherham, a real handful who was giving me a bad time. Jack saw that and ran over to me saying, 'Let me have him, just look and learn.' Jack wasn't the largest of players, but he knew what to do. We got a corner kick, and as the ball came in I heard an 'Umph.' Jack had gone in to the striker and put his nose all over his face. It was the textbook definition of a professional foul. He came over to me and said, 'If they're knocking you around, giving you any trouble, give them one of those and you'll be okay.' That lesson carried with me throughout my time in the first team.

Jack was like that with all of us. Of the youth players at the club at the time, the best was Billy Griffin, who always puzzled me. He was a slight, funny guy who used to die his hair a Doris Day shade of blonde. He'd walk into the dressing room on a Monday morning, his hair more blond that it had been on the Friday, and Peter would taunt him, 'Had your head in the bucket again Billy?'

Billy took it in his stride however, and was always up for a laugh. On Boxing Day 1953, we were due to play at Retford, and on the way to the game we stopped off at a hotel for a pre-match meal. After we'd finished, someone shouted, 'Billy! Sing us a Christmas song.' Billy immediately stood up and started singing Christmas carols while we egged him on.

Fashion choices and singing aside, Billy was a great player. He was a sniffer, who had a knack for being in the right place at the right time. Off the field it was a different story as he was unlucky to be at Wednesday in that era, particularly after John Fantham was promoted to the first team. He found it hard to get in the team for any length of time. Whenever any of the forward line got injured, he would come in, play well, and more often and not, score the important goals. He scored so many it was untrue. But then John, or whoever, would get back to fitness and Billy would make way.

I had similar problems. The outside left when I first started with Wednesday was Dennis Woodhead, who'd joined from the RAF immediately after the war. Whenever he wasn't playing, Bill Shadbolt would come in. If he didn't play, they'd bring in Peter Howells. As the years went by, the players changed. Dennis left for Chesterfield and was replaced by Albert Broadbent, but my situation remained the same.

At the suggestion of Hugh Swift, I settled into playing at centre-half. He convinced me that I could make it in the first team in that position, but again, in that central position were Ralph O'Donnell, Barry Butler and Peter Swan. Looking back it seems as if every man and his dog got a chance to play for Sheffield Wednesday before me.

*****

The A Team was another brief period for me, as I was soon promoted to the Central League to play in the reserve team. Playing in the reserves was once again a different experience. We went from small grounds with capacities in the few thousands, to playing in the grounds that the First Division teams played. They might have been empty, but that probably made them more impressive, playing in those huge empty stadiums. They were games where you might come up against current internationals who were coming back from injury, or the up and coming players who were on the verge of the first team.

I was now playing alongside some of the big players of recent times for Wednesday. Players coming back from injury, and senior players who had dropped down from the first team like Dave MacIntosh, Doug Witcomb and Ron Capewell. They were always willing to give me advice. One time I was sat in the Bolton Wanderers away dressing room with Doug. He was sat smoking in the bath, giving me an intense lecture on 'hospital' balls. 'Okay Don. Make sure you don't think about the ball. Think about the man on the other end of it,' he told me between each puff.

I looked up to Doug so I took him seriously. A 'hospital' ball was a ball passed to a stationary player who was invariably tackled from behind. The preferred pass was one that caught the player in motion, so he could immediately turn and run with the ball. 'If you see an opposition player bearing down on someone, the last thing you want to do is pass them a ball that they have to wait for, because if you do, they'll get hit,' said Doug who was gesticulating wildly. He was completely oblivious to Dave MacIntosh who had moved into position, squirted a big dollop of soap in Doug's eyes, and put out his pipe

I played in every position for the reserves at some point. One of my first games was at Old Trafford against Manchester United reserves. I invited all my friends. The whole gang, about fifteen of them, turned up and whooped and hollered from the top of the stand, jumping and swinging on the barriers. I was playing outside left and Wednesday veteran Redfern Froggatt, who was a God as far as I was concerned, was playing inside left. After a particular run of play where the ball had got away from me, I remember Redfern jogged up to me, put his hands on my shoulders and said, 'You're getting a little too excited son. Settle down.'

I even played at centre forward a couple of times, and really suffered for it. The first occasion was when we were away to Blackpool. In the net that day was George Farm, a Scottish international goalkeeper. During one move the ball was crossed in and knocked down the middle. I'd anticipated the move so decided to go for it putting all my energy into flicking the ball over to the goal without any real knowledge of who was around me. As I made contact, George Farm rushed forward and managed to punch me square in both eyes.

The second time, we were playing Newcastle up at St James' Park. In their team was a hard player called Frank Brennan who had played in Cup Finals. In similar fashion, I decided to go up for a ball. While I was watching it, Frank came in and knocked me so hard that my forehead split open. I came back down to Sheffield with a great big gash above my eye. It turned into a scar that I carry to this day. It was obvious that I lacked the awareness needed for that position. I wasn't skilful enough, and was probably too brave for my own good. I'd be jumping up for balls, concentrating solely on what I was going to do with it, rather than on who was around me.

*****

On my twenty-first birthday, I received my calling up papers for National Service among my birthday cards. I'd been assigned to the Royal Signals at Catterick in North Yorkshire. I made my way there, and the only way I could describe it was as a situation of ordered confusion. The sergeants and corporals were shouting at us to get in line to receive our kit and blankets. Then we were given our berets, which we boiled down until they fitted.

The next day, we were lined up in front of the drill sergeant who set out the routine. The order of the day was marching. Then he asked if any of us were professional sportsmen. Obviously I came forward as a footballer. He took my name down, and the officer in charge of the sports team approached me to ask what position I played. I was told that I would go into Holding Troop. This meant I'd be in the gym as a Physical Training Instructor (PTI), and would be able to travel back to play for Wednesday.

Once we'd finished square bashing, we were all put in trucks to be sent to our deployment. I was waiting to be called out for Holding Troop, when my name was called out to get into a truck bound for Gallowgate, a camp near Richmond. 'What's your name? Megson. No, you're in here.'

I was told that I was there for a two week sentry training course before being deployed to Germany. I was going to learn how to march between two sentry boxes. I tried to tell them that I should be in Holding Troop but in the army nobody listens to you. I received my sentry kit and was told to report to the gym. The very first person I saw was Peter Swan who had been made a PTI. He looked at me and a big grin spread across his face. 'If your number gets shouted out,' he said. 'You have to run around my red and black jumper three times and back.'

I had to get out of this situation, so I got on the phone to Eric Taylor and told him that I might be sent to Germany. Luckily for me, Eric knew a lot of people, and rang one of the Colonels, who in turn phoned the Lieutenant who was in charge. He told me it wasn't possible to transfer me because it would set back the rest of the training for the other men. I was back on the phone. 'Eric, he won't let me go.'

Eventually he managed to get something organised, and I was told to report back to Catterick. When my transport arrived, a lad jumped off the truck. He said to me, 'There's been a mix up, my name's Mason.'

Once that was sorted, I was assigned to a regiment. Having previously put my hand up for sport, one of the officers, Trelloney, wanted me in 1TR for the football team. To get there, I had to go for an induction examination in PTI ability. I was expected to do a gymnastic display, go over the horse, perform somersaults, hand stands and back flips. Of course, these moves weren't really a footballer's forte, but I probably had a little more of an advantage because of footballer's fitness.

Of course, the aim of the test wasn't so much to test skill, but willingness. They wanted to find out if I had the bottle to do the routines, not necessarily whether I was ready to teach off the bat. The Major turned to Bill Corbett, another of the PTI's, and shouted, 'Give me a demonstration on a head spring.' Bill was good and did one straight away. Then it was my turn. I had six attempts and still I couldn't do it. But I tried, and that was all he wanted to see.

Within a few weeks I was given my uniform, made a Lance Corporal, and transferred to 1TR. I was then sent for a two week course in Scarborough on how to stand at the front as a leader, give a presentation, and teach exercises. Then I was back to Catterick to be placed in the gym. In there with me were Rod Thomas and Geoff Dolby, who played for Hunslet Rugby Club. Our home was the equipment cupboard, which had been converted into a dorm, with the apparatus remaining in the gym.

Right from the start, life in the army became a game of counting down how many days you had left to go. Every morning we'd get up for the staff PTI session at 7.00am. Most of them were cooks, and the men who worked in the motor shop. They'd come over for breakfast and hang around in the changing rooms for an hour having a smoke before leaving for the rest of the day.

We kept up the arrangement with the early morning PTI for a while, until the Sergeant Major decided to surprise us with an early 6:00am visit. He fired us out of the gym and put us in a billet with the new recruits and made us march in full uniform for two weeks. It was the only time I did any marching, and the only time I wore my uniform apart from when I hitch-hiked.

Another man who made his way into our circle was Johnny Prescott, a middleweight boxer who later fought Henry Cooper and Billy Walker. Naturally, Johnny was on the boxing team and actually lost quite a few fights against the other soldiers because they tended to go in flailing, rather than playing it the way professionals would. We got on well, and I brought him home a couple of times to Manchester on weekends to meet my family.

I used to invite Johnny and the cooks over in the evenings to play some five-a-side football matches. One night, someone put in a shot that went wide and hit one of the pieces of apparatus, a climbing beam that was stored on a ledge. The beam dropped down behind the jumping horse making a clanking noise. It was only when we'd finished that we found that the beam had gone straight through the floor. We moved the horse backwards to cover the hole and made sure that it stayed there until we'd completed our service.

*****

In my two years in the service, I hardly missed a match for Wednesday. My telegram still arrived in the post, and I continued to commute to Sheffield on weekends. By then I was a part-time professional, paid £6 for playing football and £8 from my apprenticeship. The first team were only on £14 a week at the time so in a roundabout way, I was as well off as the full-time players.

Getting to and from Catterick was a pain. It was either put

on my uniform and hitch-hike, or catch a train. The train would arrive in Darlington at about 4.00am, and all the soldiers would sprint into the waiting room to sleep on the tables and chairs, and on the floor. If you didn't move fast enough you had to sleep outside. It was a two hour wait until the bus started running from the railway station to Catterick.

I only missed four weekends in two years, even after I was moved down to Aldershot to do an advanced PTI course. The barracks I stayed in were two miles from the gym, and in the morning I'd have to run the distance to the gym with my PTI kit under my arm. I'd do a shift in the gym, have a shower, and then run back for lunch. Then another run back for the afternoon shift before back again for tea.

Eric Taylor had arranged with 1TR for me to have Friday's off for travel, so I could get back for the games in time. Friday also happened to be six-ring boxing practice, there were six boxing rings set out in the gym. Each of them would have two fighters inside, and an instructor yelling at them what to do with their left and their right. After all the fights were over, we'd congregate around one of the rings, and the instructor would pick us out in pairs, depending on weight, and then two of those chosen would have to get in the ring.

The two men would then have to fight. Each would be cautious until the first person got hit in the face, and from then on it would be self-preservation time. After a couple of knocks, I'd remember that I would be seeing Yvonne, who wouldn't be all that keen to see me with a broken nose. I'd wade in at that point, hoping to land a few punches and get it over with as quickly as possible

As soon as I got out of the ring, I'd go into the changing rooms, and without having time for a shower, get my civvies on. Then I'd run a quarter of a mile flat out to catch the train to London, then on to Manchester to see Yvonne, and finally the train to Sheffield the next morning. Then it was back to Manchester, to spend as much time with Yvonne as I could. I could see the bus stop from Yvonne's gate, so I'd wait for it to go past and then sprint down a parallel road to pick it up on the other side of the estate. Then it would be on the bus to Catterick, and on the bus back to Aldershot.

I've always been bad at getting out of bed, and one time it counted against me. Every morning, the Sergeant would come in to wake us up. 'Right! Stand by your beds!' One Thursday, I was caught sleeping. He ordered me to clean his office that Saturday. I tried to remonstrate, telling him that I was due to travel to play for Wednesday. 'Well you won't be this weekend," he bellowed at me.

Faced with missing the game, I decided to show some mettle. I approached him later that day, and somehow swapped the punishment to the Friday. The office was an absolute tip, and it took all day to clean, scrubbing chalk lines from the cupboards and wiping the floors and the walls. I finally got off, but had to catch the midnight train to Manchester, and head on straight to Hillsborough. Little did I know that my dedication would soon start to pay off.

4

Losing End

1960-61 was my first pre-season, and by all accounts it was a fierce one. On the first day of training, Harry Catterick and Tommy Eggleston gathered us in the changing room and talked us through an enhanced training schedule they believed would elevate us to the next level of mental and physical preparedness. They wanted us to be able to chase hard all day, fight stronger and harder to get wins, and have a greater capability of turning a game in our favour, even when under pressure.

For the first few weeks the new schedule was a killer. The facilities we had at our disposal were basic, not what you envisaged for a team that wanted to challenge for the title. We would change into our kits at Hillsborough before walking a mile up the road to the Owlerton training pitch. A circuit of about fifteen activities would be set up around the pitch and we would work them in pairs – thirty seconds on and thirty seconds off. My training partner was Peter Swan. At first, we lasted a couple of times round before we were sapped of energy. But as the weeks passed by we felt ourselves getting fitter.

There were high expectations come the first day of the season. The fact that Burnley had won the title the previous season proved that it was possible for an unfancied team to get to the top. It quickly became a race between us and Tottenham for top spot, after we went eleven games unbeaten before we lost to Wolves in October. Our goal scoring was dominated by John Fantham, Bobby Craig, and Keith Ellis, with Johnny Quinn chipping in with the odd one here and there. John was becoming lethal in front of goal, getting over twenty in the league that season, with Keith right behind him.

During that run I got my game against Stanley Matthews when he played at Hillsborough for Blackpool. Before the match, Eric Taylor announced to the press that he was going to play and the gate inevitably went up. I considered it an honour to be on the same pitch as Stan. I was twenty-three, and he was in his mid-forties, but it didn't register. Stan was in the First Division and still one of the quickest players over five yards. Before the game everyone told me to wait for his second feint. That was the way to get him.

The first time we came up against each other, he had the ball, and did his thing. He did the first feint ... and he was gone. I'd made the cardinal sin of turning my back on him, and now I had no idea where he was. I turned round quickly, tripped myself up, and fell over. Everyone in the stand started laughing. 'There goes big young strong Megson,' they thought, 'Going arse-over-tit over old man Matthews.'

I wasn't having any of that. The next time the ball came to Stan, I positioned myself a little closer, and clashed with him, to try and make him work a little harder for the ball. Stan, being the age he was, didn't want to get too physical, and pulled out. After that, I didn't have any trouble keeping him under control.

I knew that England selector Bobby Shentall had been present at the Burnley match, so it didn't come as a total shock when a few days later, I received a letter informing me that I'd been chosen to represent the Football League XI in the first ever match against the Italian League. Ray Wilson, the first choice England left full-back, was renowned for his passing vision, which was my weak spot, so it was a fantastic opportunity to challenge him for his place.

Both associations took the game very seriously, and selected strong squads. I essentially played alongside the England defence. Ron Springett was in goal, and Bobby Robson, Ron Flowers, Jimmy Armfield, and Peter Swan were alongside me. The Italian team was just as strong. Lorenzo Buffon was the goalkeeper, Cesare Maldini was in defence, Antonio Angelillo, an Argentinian-Italian striker, and the great John Charles, were in attack. I was marking Kurt Hamrin, an extremely talented Swedish winger who played for Fiorentina. He was deadly.

The game began in a civil manner until Denis Law went into a strong tackle with John Charles, who went down holding his leg. 'Crampo! Crampo!' he shouted. The crowd thought that Denis had tried to injure John and went wild. They started whistling, booing, and throwing litter onto the pitch. Once they'd run out of litter they started throwing their seat cushions.

The game became a kick-up, which was the last thing I needed. The Italians were constantly body-checking us and pulling our shirts. The German referee lost control and Harry Potts, who was in charge of us that night, started to get wound up by his performance. At one point, the Italian League were awarded a free kick. They brought the ball about twenty-five yards further forward from where the foul had been committed. This was the final straw for Harry who got up from the bench, ran onto the pitch, and dashed with the ball to where he thought the free kick should be taken.

By that time, we were already two goals down. After five minutes Juan Tacchi of Napoli was passed the ball on the outside of me. I made chase with him down the left side of the box, and was just about to jockey the ball off him when he chipped it over Ron from a tight angle. Ron had to go off soon after with concussion after hitting his head in attempting to save the goal.

Just after the half hour, the Italians split our defence to let in Jose Altafini, the Brazilian inside left, who shot at Bert Trautmann. Bert could only deflect the ball to the other side of the box where Hamrin powered past me to score from the rebound. Altafini scored two more goals in the second half. Denis Law and Peter McParland got two consolation goals for us. Final score 4-2, and not the glory fixture that I had envisaged.

On the way out of the stadium the Italian fans, still incensed at Denis, threw stones at us. We all had to duck for cover, with our heads inside our coats, and rush to the coach. We were ferried to a hotel where a lavish banquet had been laid on. All the Football

League players were sat on one side of the table, with the Italian League facing them, while the dignitaries and the referees were sat up at the top.

We were tucking into our main course when Denis Law, who was a bit of a joker, decided that he was getting bored of all the civility. He leant forward in his seat, looked one way and the other, and grabbed a daffodil from one of the vases in the middle of table. Without flinching he bit the head off it, chewed slowly, and started smirking at all the Italians. We were laughing our heads off.

The next day, we returned to the airport. We got on the plane and everything went smoothly until five minutes after take-off, when the pilot came over the intercom and stated that we'd had to turn around. Apparently there was a fault with the electrics that was giving the pilots false information so we found ourselves sat back in the departure lounge. Bert, who was a studious man, was reading a book. Denis, again bored, took the book off him, ripped out the last page, and started eating it. I was sat at the other end of the room, and all I could hear was Bert, in his heavy German accent shouting, 'You bloody nuisance.'

*****

I was back at Hillsborough the next week for a friendly against Georgian side Dinamo Tbilisi. Bill Nicholson was at the ground to assess us for the next league game which was home to Tottenham. The Tbilisi line up consisted of students and civil servants, and standing on the pitch waiting for their national anthem to begin, both teams were unaware that the copy of the Soviet national anthem they'd brought with them had broken. We were stood around waiting for the tune to pipe up, but all that came out was static and wind.

Due to his concussion Ron was missing for the game, so Roy McLaren took over in goal. It didn't stop us thrashing them 6-0. Roy kept his place for the next game. It was November 14th, 1960. This was the big one, exactly a year on from my début.

Tottenham had all the momentum – they'd scored over fifty goals and dropped only one point so far that season. But for all the talent of John White, Bobby Smith and Terry Dyson, we somehow managed to keep a clean sheet, and Roy pulled off save after save. Hillsborough roared that night, enough to make the hairs on the back of your neck stand on end. Harry Catterick's advice was, 'Score more goals than Tottenham do.'

The first half had plenty of chances but no goals. At half time, Harry Catterick decided that Alan Finney and Billy Griffin should swap wings to confuse the Tottenham full backs. Just after we came out, Roy made a great save after Peter hit a poor back pass that Bobby Smith had leapt onto. The ball was cleared up field to Bobby Craig, who whipped it into the box for Billy Griffin to slot home.

Maurice Norman equalised with a header, but with about twenty minutes to go, the ball came to me in defence and I hit it as hard as I could up into the penalty area. Keith Ellis was making himself really big in the box and he managed to get the ball to Johnny Fantham who scored in front of the Kop.

Tottenham took the defeat very badly. I'd tackled Les Allen hard at one stage, and he tried to get me booked. After the final whistle, Billy went to shake hands with Peter Baker who first ignored him, then kicked him in the ankle. As we left the pitch, Billy Nicholson shook a clenched fist at Harry.

It was disappointing that after such a great performance we went on a poor run of three defeats. We lost to Leicester and Aston Villa, and then to Everton. If it wasn't for those results we might have stood a better chance of taking the title, because after that we went nineteen games unbeaten. Our defence was getting meaner and tighter. Peter Johnson and I were forging a great understanding alongside Peter Swan, Tony Kay and Tom McAnearney.

Peter had previously played for Rotherham, and had been tracked by Wednesday for years after he impressed during a friendly between the Sheffield and Hallamshire FA and Glasgow. Wednesday had offered Rotherham the record fee for a full back at the time, but Peter had turned it down. In 1957 they finally persuaded him to make the move to Sheffield.

Peter had played all over the pitch, even at centre forward, but like me had been moved to full-back by Harry. He never fully came to terms with being restricted to one position however, believing that players had to be innovative and willing to adapt to other situations in games. He had clear ideas about how the game should be played, and was a real stickler for details. In the dressing room after matches he'd be saying, 'Well the ball was about one and a half feet from the side of me, so I wasn't able to get it. And then there was this little incident which prevented me from doing this. And don't forget about that Don.'

We were once playing Aston Villa at home getting pulled all over the place. They had a corner and for some reason, I found myself covering the back post as the ball came in, although Peter usually covered that area. I accidentally handled the ball to give a penalty, but the press wrote it as if Peter had been the one who gave it away. He cornered me the following day, and demanded that I go to the press to clarify that it wasn't him. He'd always start wagging his finger when he was aggrieved, but all I could do on that occasion was smirk, 'I'm quite happy for you to take the blame for that one Peter.'

Our team was the exact opposite to Tottenham. We were assembled on a shoestring, and you've got to give credit to Eric Taylor for that. Apart from Bobby Craig, we'd all been purchased under his watch, and the majority of us had come straight from non-league. Tottenham's players on the other hand, were expensive, and they carried themselves in a way that spoke 'We're superior to you.' To them, we were 'the guys from up north' who didn't have the skill or class to compete. Being London players, they were caught up in the night life and the élan of Carnaby Street and Knightsbridge.

In all honesty I couldn't say that we were envious. Sheffield was a great, friendly city, and the country was looking to us as underdogs. We didn't see it quite like that as we knew that we carried a lot of armour to beat people. But it was useful to be underestimated at times. And in Bobby Craig, we had the bargain of the season. He didn't look like a footballer. He was stumpy and stocky and only about five foot six, but he could change direction very quickly and had great dribbling skills. He was a good foil for John Fantham who was fast and direct, even though he could blow hot and cold.

Bobby was very cocky, thought quite highly of himself, and would get in to scraps at the drop of a hat. He wasn't the best looking lad, but he thought of himself as a bit of a man about town, and was always out in Sheffield trying to pull girls. I was out with him once and told him, 'Do you ever notice that whenever you go abroad you can't pull anything? You've got no chance of pulling girls when you leave Sheffield.' It didn't stop him though. He was a wild man.

He and Tom McAnearney had plenty of disagreements. Once at Fulham, Bobby was complaining that Tom wasn't giving him the ball. Bobby had a tendency to stand still and wait for the ball until it reached him. Tom recognised this as 'hospital' ball territory, but Bobby didn't see it that way. Tom remonstrated initially, but finally gave in and passed him the ball. Eddie Lowe immediately rushed into him and whacked him to the floor. All the way home he complained that Tom had set him up for a fall.

Tom was a fiery lad. Both he and his brother Jim had taken their coaching badges early, and I think this played against both of them when it came to dealing with managers like Harry. I believed my role in the team was to get the ball back from the opposition, and pass it to the players who could move the ball on. And that's what I did. I was always willing to have a go but if I felt that it wasn't working out, I would get the ball to someone who could do the job.

Tommy, on the other hand, wanted to pass the ball and create chances. Even when he wasn't on his game he would still want to hit the killer passes. Not to criticise him, because he had great vision, but he'd be giving the ball away, and wouldn't have the pace to get the ball back. I used to ask him to ease up a little by telling him to play it simple instead of wanting the ball off everyone.

He had a heart as big as a bucket though. He'd be shouting his head off, wanting the ball from the goalkeeper in the six-yard box, and it wouldn't always come off for him but the fans loved him for it. However it didn't stop Harry from stripping him of the captaincy. We were playing against Birmingham and Harry had asked him to kick Johnny Gordon, who was their inside right. At half time Harry marched up to him, 'I thought I told you to kick Johnny Gordon.'

'Look,' replied Tom. 'He's doing nothing. I know Gordon. If I kick him, he'll kick me. And it'll end as a kick-up. Someone might get injured.'

At that moment, Tony Kay piped up, 'Leave it to me boss. I'll give him what you want.' Harry went on to make Tony the new captain. You could tell that Tom was disappointed. It was from then on that Tony came into vogue.

*****

In November, right in the middle of one of our good runs, we lost against Aston Villa at Hillsborough. Harry was fuming. After the match he got everyone in the dressing room and started to rub his hands together, which he always did when he was about to talk to you. 'Right, that was absolutely disgraceful. You will all be in tomorrow for training. And you will all play in the reserves on Monday.'

Ron Springett put his hand up, 'I'm not coming in. I go home after matches.'

Harry was not used to being talked back to, 'You will be here tomorrow. You will train.'

When Ron had signed for Wednesday he had agreed with Eric Taylor that he could stay in London. He would catch the Master Cutler train on Friday, train with us a little, and then play on the Saturday. I can honestly say that it was never a problem. Ron knew exactly how we played, and Peter and I had great communication with him. With this in mind, Ron wasn't finished. 'I'll go over your head Harry,' he said, meaning that he'd go and squeal to Eric.

'You do that Ron, and you'll never play in my team again,' replied Harry.

Ron crumbled. He stayed in Sheffield overnight and trained the next day. On the Monday, we all played in the reserves at

Blackpool. Not long after that, Ron received a message telling him to travel to Sheffield on the Thursday rather than the Friday. He was tailed by reporters in London and also when he got to Sheffield. When he arrived at the stadium, he was ushered into a board meeting. At the meeting, Eric made Harry apologise to Ron in front of everyone. Harry must have felt so undermined, but Ron was Wednesday's big England star and carried a lot of weight.

Just before Christmas I was dropped from the team for a game against West Brom. It was a midweek game and the first of three games in a row that we drew – games that we should have won. Unusually, the team hadn't been picked beforehand but I travelled with the team as normal. I walked into the dressing room, took off my coat and put it on to the peg next to the number 3 shirt, sat down, and started reading the match programme. Harry walked in, looked at me and said, 'You're not in the side. I'm playing Brian Hill instead.' There was no warning, no words, I was dropped, and there was no recourse.

The next game was a home match against Arsenal. Brian played again and we drew 1-1. I was asked to play in the reserves, which I did, and after the match I went to speak to Harry about the situation. I knocked on Harry's door and walked in. Even before I'd said anything he looked up and said, 'You are the best left back in this club, now go out and prove it.' I turned around, and walked out without him saying another word.

I was back in the team for the next match on Boxing Day. We travelled down on Christmas evening and stayed the night in London, the usual routine. The next day we played the game and got another 1-1 draw with a goal from Keith Ellis. Manchester City were also playing in London that day, so Derek Wilkinson and I decided to go home on their supporters train.

On the coach back to Sheffield, the players were in high spirits, and apparently the drink was flowing. Travelling with the first team was a young inside-forward called Doug McMillan. It was common practice for a young player to travel with the team to get experience. The coach was driving up the A1 and they'd just got to Huntingdon when the driver lost control and hit a bridge.

Several of the players were injured. Peter Swan broke his collar bone and was thrown through the air. Tom McAnearney was able to get out through the emergency exit and, for some reason he was never able to remember, grabbed hold of a travel rug and ran up the inside shoulder.

Doug had been fiddling around with the radio and singing with Johnny Quinn when the coach crashed, and somehow got his leg trapped in the wreckage. Luckily there was a doctor driving behind us, who told him that if they didn't get him out of there quickly he would die from lack of circulation. So it was decided that the leg had to be amputated. All the way through the procedure Doug sang 'Scotland the Brave.'

And he was brave. A benefit match was arranged at Hillsborough against a Select XI, and before the kickoff, Doug walked on to the pitch with Derek Dooley. Doug was fortunate in a way because unlike Derek, he had his leg taken off below the knee, meaning he had a stump and could still run and walk relatively easily. He ended up going to Lilleshall to do his coaching badge. I was there once as a staff coach taking a session, and I saw him. He'd work and train all day until his stump was red raw, but the next day he'd be back out there doing sessions.

Alan Finney and Peter Johnson had also been able to get a direct train to Doncaster, so had not been on the coach. After a night out on the town, oblivious to what had happened, they returned home as normal. It was only the next morning that Alan was confronted by his wife. 'Why were you late last night'?

'FOG,' Alan responded. 'A pea souper!'

'What about this then?' She threw the newspaper down on the table, with the story plastered on the front page and asked him to explain. I never found out how he managed to get out of that one.

*****

We had to do without Peter Swan for two months after Christmas. Taking his place was Ralph O'Donnell, a first team player in the mid-1950s who had been in competition with Peter to be the successor to Don McEvoy. At his best, he'd been on the fringes of the England squad, but had given up full-time football to become a teacher. He still played in the reserves, and stepped back in every now and again when Peter was on England duty.

In February I finally moved to Sheffield. In many ways, it was a relief as commuting from Manchester every day was getting tedious. At the time, it was a common thing for football clubs to purchase housing stock and Wednesday had recently bought houses on Butler Street in Stannington. Peter Swan had arranged to move into one, and a few weeks previously he'd asked me if I was interested in renting the other.

The night before I moved we played Manchester United in the FA Cup. We'd beaten Leeds 2-0 in the third round, and had drawn with United 1-1 at Hillsborough. We travelled to United and gave them their biggest defeat in a quarter of a century. Harry Gregg and David Gaskell were both out injured, so Ronnie Briggs, a seventeen-year-old youth goalkeeper came in. The match was Bobby Craig's first game since before Christmas and he ran the show. We went ahead after two minutes with John Fantham wading through their entire defence before Mark Pearson equalised. A hard drive from Alan Finney that bounced off Briggs' arms put us back in front, and then a Keith Ellis header from a Derek Wilkinson free kick and a second Ellis strike put us 4-1 by half time.

In the second half, John got another, and Keith got his hat trick before Alan finished them off with a header from a Bobby Craig cross. I remember the United fans fleeing Old Trafford in their droves. It was the rarest sight I ever saw. I stayed at home overnight and moved the next day. The delivery men loaded up the removal van, and then I hitched a lift with them to Sheffield.

We'd gone eight matches unbeaten, and were all set to go on another substantial cup run, but Burnley saw to that in the fifth round. Ralph O'Donnell had done so well that he didn't warrant being dropped, and with Peter still struggling, he continued to shine. We drew 0-0 at Hillsborough, and were beaten 2-0 at Turf Moor. On March 25th we played Manchester United again at Hillsborough, setting a new record of fifteen unbeaten games.

It was another crushing win for us, with Gerry Young scoring another great hat trick. But after that we drew three games in a row, an away game at Blackburn 1-1, and two home games, one to Newcastle 1-1 and one to Leicester 2-2. In fact, we only won once in the last seven.

There were constant stories coming out in the newspapers of Harry Catterick being linked with other clubs. First it was Liverpool, then Leeds, Leicester, and Nottingham Forest. Though Harry claimed at one point that he didn't want to leave Sheffield, he'd certainly proven by that point that he had what it took to build a Championship winning side, and it was well know that he didn't see eye to eye with Eric Taylor's emphasis on improving the ground.

Eric Taylor thought about stadium design deeply and wanted Hillsborough to be a first class venue. It was a lot different back then. You had the Ozzie Owl Club. For the 1966 World Cup they built the restaurant which was up a pair of wrought iron stairs next to the player's entrance. Then there was the drying room where they used to have all the laundry hanging over racks. Close to the end of his career, Norman Curtis used to put on a rubber suit and do his training in there in the damp.

Round the back of the stadium was a piece of open ground where we did our Friday warm up. We'd start off there and do laps around the stadium, which was more open plan back then. After the team was announced, we would come back and play head tennis and do a few stretches before heading home.

Harry was of the belief that investment in the ground had come at the cost of other things. He wanted investment in training facilities as we had no gym and the reserve teams were still practising on the Owlerton dog track some days. I remember him saying to me, just before he left, 'That Taylor, he's got a six foot wall round him, and I couldn't un-lodge one brick.'

Harry had been tracking Joe Baker, a hot young English striker from Hibernian, for over a year. I would never decry Keith Ellis because he'd flourished under Harry, but it was obvious that Joe would have brought an extra dimension to our attack. Instead of relying on knock-ons from Keith to Bobby Craig and John Fantham, Joe would have allowed us to bring the ball down more in the penalty area. Whether it was because of wages or the transfer fee, the board never came to an agreement. He eventually signed for Torino, and then for Arsenal.

Just before the Tottenham game, Harry made his move. I wouldn't say I was upset, because it never feels like that. But I was disappointed. He'd been my first manager, and he had helped me improve my game a lot. One by one, we were called in the office where he told us individually of his departure, and wished us the best of luck. Though he initially denied having another job lined up, he took over at Everton a week later. Eric Taylor took over as caretaker.

There was a brilliant atmosphere for the return game at Tottenham. The gap between us had been reduced to two points and we were still in with a chance. We had to win to stay in it, because Tottenham had scored so many goals. Unfortunately, we were missing Tom McAnearney, who had travelled up to Dundee to be with his mother before she passed away.

Within thirty minutes we were ahead, and it happened that I was the scorer. John Fantham got floored by a Tony Norman tackle, and we got a free kick. I was up to take it. I hit the wall with my first effort, but smashed the rebound past Bill Brown. It was my first professional goal for Wednesday. I always ran to celebrate with goal scorers, so it was a great feeling to have everyone running to me instead.

Moments later, we could have gone further ahead, when Keith Ellis headed against the post. But that woke Tottenham up. Trevor Dyson out-jumped me on a cross and managed to get the ball to Bobby Smith. He went right round Peter Swan before slotting it in. A minute later it was 2-1. Spurs got a free kick which Danny Blanchflower hit to Les Allen, who volleyed home. We'd lost the title in a two minute flurry.

*****

That summer we headed to Nigeria. Like all the tours we went on, the trip was down to Eric Taylor's influence. In his office was a map of the world with red dots showing where Sheffield Wednesday had played, and black dots where he wanted to take us. Nigeria was a real experience. We played three games around the country, and the weather was roasting for the duration.

Because he'd played so well for us that season, Ralph O'Donnell was invited to come with us on the trip. He accepted, and the decision led to him getting sacked from his teaching job. Two days before we were due to fly out, the Local Education Authority stated that he was no longer allowed to go, but he came anyway.

Our first match was against a Western Region XI in Ibaden. We checked into the hotel which was nice enough, but basic. The pace of life over there was so totally removed from ours. In the evenings, we drank in a place called The Dressler Bar, which wasn't a pretty sight. Sewerage was flowing down the street and you had to walk over it on two planks to get through the entrance of the bar.

From Ibaden we headed south to Lagos to play the NFA Eagles. In the middle of the pitch was a massive flag pole set in concrete, and our dressing room was a workman's hut made of steel, with benches stuck to the walls. During the match, Tommy Eggleston threw lumps of ice onto the pitch for us to pick up and cool down. It was the only time that I chose ice blocks over a game. Bobby Craig played really well, but Billy Griffin wouldn't stay out on his wing. I asked him what the problem was and it turned out there was a lizard on that part of the pitch, and as far as he was concerned it was a no go area.

The following day, we were invited by Lord Head (the British High Commissioner to Lagos) to travel on his yacht to Victoria Island, situated in Lagos Lagoon. At the time it was fairly undeveloped and there was no jetty, so the boat had to stop about twenty feet from the shore. I wasn't that good a swimmer, but I just about managed it from a diving start. Swimming back I couldn't get any speed at all, and the other guys in front of me were slowing me down. I couldn't tread water, so I started going under. I thought I was a goner, but Ralph O'Donnell grabbed me by the hair and pulled me back up.

The beach was beautiful, and we all got settled into sunbathing. Alan Finney positioned himself not far from me. All of a sudden, he jolted upright and started screaming. Insects were a given in that part of the world, but this one was monstrous. Alan jumped up and starting sprinting down the beach, with the insect giving chase. Keith Ellis, who was bobbing just off the shore, decided to take action. He whacked his surfboard in the direction of the hornet and it flew out of his hands and into the sea. Whether he succeeded in getting the hornet we'll never know.

We left Lagos and travelled across country to play the Eastern Region in Enugu. Our chosen driver was slowly chewing a root that made his teeth red, and before we set off, the Dutch woman who was in charge of our group marched up to the front of the bus and shouted, 'Get out.' The driver got out from the vehicle. She pointed at another man who was waiting at the side of the road. 'Can you drive?' she asked.

'Yes.'

Then get in and drive!'

All along the way down the highway were wrecked cars and small communities living out of huts. Once we arrived in Enugu, we were told not to go out in the sun. Colin Dobson however, decided he was going to go out anyway to try and get a tan. Having red hair and fair skin, it wasn't the best thing to do. Halfway through the match, Colin jumped up to head the ball into their net for our first goal. All the skin came off his forehead and took a ride into the net with the ball. There were loads of petty fouls all the way through the match, and eventually, punches started to be thrown about. The police had to clear the pitch in the end.

The last game was in Kano against the Northern Region. Stopping off overnight, we slept in little individual huts. Even at night, it was steaming hot, and there were insects everywhere. There was also a type of lizard called the Red Headed Agama which had a black body and used to bounce around in front of you as you walked. They were sticking to the walls of the huts and getting everywhere. Come night time, I heard a knocking on my door. 'Meg! Meg.'

'Who's that?' I called.

'Meg. Can I get in with you?'

It was Billy. The lizards had got to him again.

5

Hobos

Vic Buckingham looked an unlikely candidate to be a football manager when I first met him. He dressed in a tweed jacket with a big floral handkerchief sticking out of the top pocket, and topped himself off with a trilby hat. When he spoke about football, all exuberant language and talk of the beautiful game and with his arms waving around, he looked like he belonged in a West End revue rather than a dugout.

Behind that mask however, lay a highly intelligent man, steeped in football. You only had to look at his CV to discover that he was a very talented manager with an intimate knowledge of football tactics. His previous post had been at Ajax Amsterdam, where he'd won the Dutch League. Before that he'd taken West Brom to an FA Cup Final and finished high up the table.

Vic had been on Eric's radar for over a year. The previous summer, when rumours of Harry's future had first got out, Vic had been strongly linked with the Wednesday job. He was conscious of his son's education – while Vic and his wife and two daughters were in Amsterdam, his son was living with relatives in London. Vic chose to remain in Amsterdam another year, but Eric kept in touch and after Harry left, Eric invited Vic to be his guest at the Tottenham away game. Though Vic had already agreed to take over at Plymouth, the lure of Wednesday proved too great.

Having been away from the English scene for three years, Vic knew he was under considerable pressure to replicate the success of the previous season, or risk being thought of as the wrong choice. Losing Harry had been a blow to the fans, and I think they had expectations of Vic being from the same side of town. What they got was the complete opposite!

Vic had an infectious outlook on life. He was a purist. Football was an art form and it had to be treated as such. Not only did he expect us to play attractive football with guile and finesse, and for us to knock the ball with intelligence round the whole pitch, he also wanted us to enjoy ourselves. 'Okay gentlemen,' he used to tell us before we went down the tunnel. 'Play attractive football. Give the crowd something to cheer about and get your foot in to the ball.'

Looking back, it's no surprise that Vic is considered one of the architects of 'Total Football.' He tried to instil the positive philosophy in us day after day. It was a long way from Harry who'd been a basics man. 'Forget the enjoyment,' he'd have said, 'Just get them beat.'

The Ajax connection proved lucrative. For about five years after Vic joined Wednesday we went over to Holland to play friendlies, make use of their facilities, and explore Amsterdam. It is a wonderful city. Thousands of buildings line its canals and cobbled streets, with elegant bridges criss-crossing the expanse of the water. Vic was in his element because he knew everyone, and knew the language.

Ajax had a fantastic set up, even then. Their main stand had two sides to it. One side faced the pitch and the other overlooked the training facilities. There was a large hut on the side of the compound that contained footballs and bibs. Local children were encouraged to come to the ground to play games and then to put the equipment away. It was obvious that as soon as they turned professional, the Dutch would be a force in the game.

The first time we visited that summer, we took the opportunity to sample night life. Vic set us an evening curfew which we missed by about ten minutes. We arrived back at the hotel to find Vic waiting in the lobby, fully dressed with trilby hat on, tapping his foot on the marble floor. 'You're all fined,' he said bluntly. 'You broke curfew.'

John Frye, one of the younger players travelling with us, stepped forward and started complaining that it had only been five minutes after all. Vic paused. He looked John up and down, and then said: 'Shut up and stand back ... you hobo.'

John was livid. 'Who the hell are you calling a hobo?

'I'm calling you a hobo, and I'm doubling your fine!'

John quickly stood down. 'Hey, I'm a hobo.'

*****

The 1961-62 season began for me with the opening of the North Stand. We won our first match away to West Brom, but the first home game against Bolton was the real event. Stanley Rous, the President of FIFA, was accepted as the guest of honour for a reception at the Grand Hotel, complete with brass band. Then on to the ground. When we took to the pitch for the first time I remember seeing the stand, full to capacity, with the national flags fluttering from the standards on the roof. It was breathtaking and Bobby Craig got the honour of scoring the first goal.

Even at that early stage, the fans recognised our change in style. With Harry in charge, we'd played a fast moving long ball game, but now we played with alternate bursts of energy, changing the pace of the game to conserve energy and to play the opposition out of their comfort zone. It took some getting used to. Throughout those early months Vic spent a lot of his time lamenting the fact that he didn't have a striker talented enough to get the ball and make his attacking strategies work fluently. Although Keith Ellis was still amongst the goals, it quickly became obvious that Vic didn't really fancy him.

We led the table at the start of September, but faded. By the time we visited West Ham, Vic had fallen out with Bobby Craig, who'd been transfer listed. We were initially on the back foot, and Ian Crawford was giving me a lot of hassle. But we eventually went ahead through Billy Griffin. West Ham equalised through a John Bond penalty, but before half time, we were back in front. Tom McAnearney found Alan Finney with a long return pass, and Alan crossed in a high floating ball that confused everyone in the box, apart from me. Looking around, I knew I had all the time in the world to tap it in. So I decided to be a bit fancy. I volleyed the ball as hard as I could and smashed the net. The game settled down, and we managed to get another goal thanks to Billy.

The highlight of the season was our run in the Inter-Cities Fairs Cup. The competition had been created in the mid-1950s by Swiss pools supremo Ernst Thommen as a way of promoting international trade fairs. Apart from our league position, Eric Taylor most likely had an influence over getting Wednesday involved. Matt Busby had been one of the first English managers to realise how lucrative European matches could be, and Eric wanted us to follow suit. He had contacts at big clubs all around Europe and tried to organise games against clubs like Barcelona, Benfica and Paris St. Germain. They were great times.

We were drawn against Olympique Lyonnais in the first round. Our flight took in Paris and Geneva, and a three hour coach drive to Lyon. Arrangements had been made for us to stay in a five star hotel but when we arrived, we found that we'd not been booked in. We were ushered down the street to one of those small side street places. There was no food and no Lyon club officials in sight. Eric being Eric, wanting only the best for the club, managed to persuade one of the best restaurants in town to open up for us, so we could have a good meal.

That was the power Eric had. He was a singularly capable man who could smooth a storm in two minutes. In that respect he was a politician. He had the right thing to say to everyone he met, and carried himself with the confidence of a man long in his position. Nobody ever knew what he was thinking until he'd made a decision, and he'd always thought things out so thoroughly that there was never any way to question his decisions.

We trained the next day and were given a tour round a local whisky distillery, whilst the stadium workers erected the temporary stand at the Stade de Gerland. It was a huge stadium, one of the old style ones with a running track. Scattered around the outside were swimming pools and other training pitches.

We were beaten 4-2 on a steaming hot night. Lyon had a strong team at the time and went three ahead with goals from Eugene

Njo-Lea and Angel Rambert. In the second half we managed to get two back from Keith Ellis and Gerry Young, but Lyon retreated into their shell and somehow managed to get another in the last minute from Nestor Combin.

John Fantham was back up front for us for the return leg, one of the greatest matches I ever played in. After about five minutes we managed to go one down, but John equalised soon after. We were awarded a free kick about midway into their half. I took it and hit the ball right into the centre and he was able to get on the end to send a looping header right over Claude Hugues' head. Just before half time Billy Griffin put us in front. In the second half he got another from an Alan Finney cross, and then Tom McAnearney scored a penalty. Lyon hit one back through Jean Djorkaeff, but a diving header from a Tony Kay free kick gave John another one. We'd managed to claw it back to 7-6 on aggregate.

Next up were Roma. The first leg was at Hillsborough, and we gave them a 4-0 hiding in front of a full house. Alan Finney had one of the best games I ever saw him play. John managed to get another goal after slotting under Fabio Cudicini, before Gerry Young, standing in at centre forward, scored a hat trick. His first goal was the best, a great combo move between Tony Kay and Derek Wilkinson led to Derek darting down the line to give a through ball to Gerry who got the perfect opening.

The second half was a scrap. I got elbowed in the face, and Tony Kay had a running battle with midfielder Francisco Lojacono who was sent off. I remember Tony running around remonstrating with the referee saying, 'Those Italians are nothing but gangsters' The fighting escalated to such a pitch that Stanley Rous issued a Fair Play Warning for the second leg and travelled personally to the Olympic Stadium in Rome.

When we arrived we were directed to the training ground, which was encircled by a high wire fence and statues of Hercules. We started kicking balls around, which attracted the Italian fans who began congregating by the fence. They recognised Tony from the press coverage and started shouting 'El Bruto' Tony didn't like the attention so he got hold of a ball and smashed it into the fence as hard as he could. I think that only enforced what the Italians thought of him.

We were beaten one-nil in the game through a last minute Peter Swan own goal, but went through on aggregate. The Roma President was shocked to learn just how little money Wednesday's team had cost to build, and was impressed enough with Bobby Craig to inquire about signing him. The match had been a riot all the way through, and it got worse after the whistle. There was a big altercation with the Roma captain, Giacomo Losi, punching Bobby in the face. The crowd rioted.

Next came Barcelona. It had snowed heavily in Sheffield, and before the match fans helped clear the pitch, with Vic and his assistant Gordon Clark also helping out. They were hard at work when the Barcelona party arrived, and after we met them we examined the pitch and had a snowball fight with the German referee.

On the night, Barcelona went ahead when Ramon Villaverde skinned me and shot past Ron into the near post. On the half hour, Colin Dobson weaved across the pitch, drawing the defenders out, before passing the ball to Gerry Young. He whipped it in and John got his head to it to make it 1-1. The Brazilian Macedo put us behind again when he chipped Ron from twenty yards, but Alan Finney then equalised with a long drive.

Then we managed to get a winner. John found Alan, who squared it to Robin Hardy, a youth player who was playing in the place of Peter Swan. He teed it up as if to shoot, but then slotted the ball through to John who managed to slot it home.

Going to Spain, we were all confident of advancing through to the semi-final. We booked into the Avenida Palace Hotel and had evening dinner with the organisers of the Barcelona Fair. One of the travelling directors was Keith Gardiner, and every time we travelled somewhere he treated one of the players to a special gift. On this occasion it was my turn, so he gave me some money and I went shopping with Peter. We were walking through the shopping arcade when I noticed this brown suede jacket. I loved it to pieces. Peter seemed to agree. 'Oh yes, that's good that, that's nice, it looks great on you Meg' he said, with a serious look on his face.

As we returned to the hotel, Peter bolted off up the steps to find the rest of the players. "Eye fellas. Meg's just bought a cowboy jacket. It's got tassels all the way down the arms. He looks like Hop-a-Long Sing!' I walked in without knowing what he'd said, and everyone started laughing and calling me the Lone Ranger, and asking me where the tassels were.

The Nou Camp is an outstanding stadium. I remember looking up at the wooden roof as we walked on the pitch, and the 90,000 capacity, and thinking that it was as good as it could get. Barcelona had a reputation of being a highly technical and tactical side. The stadium buzzed and hummed with excitement, and we played really well in spite of a 2-0 defeat. Robin Hardy stuck to Sandor Kocsis like a leach, but their attackers were just better than us. The first goal, scored by Evaristo, came after both Peter Johnson and Peter Swan had tried to clear a cross. The second was scored by Kocsis. Vincente, their winger, crossed in a ball and I only managed to half head it away. Kocsis was immediately up against me and got the ball in the net.

I think we were successful that season because we had a different style of play to the continental players. British teams, tired of opposition efforts to play short passing football, wanted to get the ball back in order to play it with purpose, and tippy tappy passing was not what most crowds want to see. It sounds a cliché, but they really did enjoy the muscular long ball game. They wanted clashes, they wanted tackles, and they wanted wingers running up the flank knocking in crosses. A long forty yard pass that by-passed the midfield, if successfully executed, was just as impressive as a short ball passing combination.

*****

After shining so brightly in the European games, Bobby Craig fell out with Vic again and was dropped to the reserves, with a transfer away from Wednesday expected. Just before he left for Blackburn Rovers in March he played in a reserve game at Manchester City. I decided to travel with the squad and take my dad to see a game at Maine Road. As I boarded the coach,

Bobby warned me, 'Watch this. I'll get away. I'll get away. This is how you do it.' We boarded, and instead of sitting at the back with all the other players, he sat in the seat immediately behind the chairman Andrew Stephen, and started to rant about all the failings of the club. 'What a bleeding club this is. They couldn't organise a piss-up in the brewery.' He ranted and raved for the entirety of the journey.

Bobby was absolutely brilliant in the game. During one move he received the ball in the eighteen-yard box, dropped his shoulder and beat a City player. Then he beat another one, and another one after that, and rounded the goalkeeper. Running towards the empty net, he brought the ball back out, then back in, waiting for the goalkeeper to get up and recover his positioning, and then popped it into the net. It was absolutely brilliant. Then it was back on the coach, and back into the same seat for the return journey. After about five minutes he started complaining again. Two days later he was gone, replaced by Colin Dobson who made the step up from the reserves.

It was only when Eddie Holliday arrived from Middlesbrough on transfer deadline day that our form recovered. After two draws against West Ham and Manchester United, we travelled to Cardiff. Peter Swan and Ron Springett were both injured, so Roy McLaren and Ralph O'Donnell stepped back in. Peter Johnson and I had their wingers Danny McCarthy and Peter King sewn up, so it was a rare opportunity for me to go roaming. I'd gone close two or three times before I scored with a thirty-five yard drive past Graham Vearncombe.

Neither Colin nor Eddie were imposing players, and they both took flack from the fans for not committing to enough tackles. It was true that neither of them liked being kicked, but I think fans failed to understand that they played in 'kickable' positions, and were therefore vulnerable to injuries. On the odd occasions that I played on the wing, I'd receive the ball and invariably someone would come in behind me and kick me up in the air and I remember thinking, 'I don't like that.' The psyche of a winger and a full back is a two-way street. If you're on the ball for too long, you'll get whacked. But if you give them too much room then they'll skin you and go on a run.

Out of the two, I think Colin was the better player. He was from Eston in Yorkshire, and like me had a fairly long wait to get in the first team. He'd been at Wednesday for six years but had wanted to complete a shipbuilding apprenticeship. He had a magic left foot, really great ball control skills, and could embarrass opposition players when he wanted to, delivering exquisite crosses every time. I remember once at Burnley when his innocence got the better of him. He'd really struggled in the first half against the Burnley full back John Angus so Vic confronted him in the dressing room. 'Colin, I don't think Angus has broken sweat against you today.'

Colin replied, 'You know boss, I don't think I have either.'

Vic was fuming, he took off his trilby and threw it to the floor in disgust.

Eddie played a different kind of game and was always more direct. He was only twenty-two, had pace, and could run with the ball. I never played that many games with him, but his best days had come at Middlesbrough. He was one of those players who had everything except desire. He'd come alive in games and disappear just as quickly. After a particularly close game against Birmingham, I remember Vic telling him, 'You're amazing you. All of your ten team-mates have fought all afternoon to win the ball and get a result, and you suddenly pop up in the ninetieth minute, score, and come off a hero.'

Off the pitch Eddie was a character and really good company on a night out. His main pleasure was gambling, particularly dog racing. He knew all the trainers at Owlerton, and would take me to watch the racing most Thursdays. He'd always be flicking through the form book in the dressing room, and he'd quickly point out two names to you. 'This one or that one?' he would ask. Invariably, I would pick the loser and him the winner.

Eddie's arrival failed to settle Vic's nerves too much. After the Cardiff match we lost three out of four, which really put our title hopes out of reach, and Vic lashed out in the local press accusing us of lacking the skill to succeed. This naturally led to a debate over whether his methods were right for the club, and whether it was right for a manager to publicly criticise his players. Rightly or wrongly it seemed to work, because we won our last four matches, but it was disappointing to all of us that we weren't able to replicate the performance of the previous season.

*****

Over the summer, Vic attempted to strengthen the side, but was only able to bring in one major signing. Luckily, he got what he and Wednesday wanted, a striker. He wasn't Joe Baker but David Layne, a £16,000 signing from Bradford City who had a notable future. He was a Sheffield lad who'd played with John Fantham for Sheffield Boys, but had never been picked up by a local side. He'd moved to Bradford where he'd scored forty-four goals in sixty-three games. It was Gordon Clark, Vic's assistant, who persuaded Vic that he could make the step up. Gordon had known Vic at West Brom, where he was nominally his assistant before taking over as manager after Vic went to Ajax.

Vic also made changes to the coaching team. In came Jack Mansell, who'd played for Cardiff and Portsmouth, and had been a contemporary of Vic in Holland, coaching Blauw-Wit Amsterdam who were known as 'The Blue Whites.' Apart from managing against each other, they used to meet up socially and they were equally inspired by progressive coaching techniques.

Spurred on by this, Vic began holding extra afternoon training sessions in an effort to improve our ball skills. In particular, he spent time with Keith Ellis, trying to improve his trapping ability. This rankled with some of the players who were used to finishing at 12.30pm, but we got used to it fairly quickly. We started playing bowls in Hillsborough Park, and when the seasons turned we'd have lunch at the Squirrel, a café just up from the stadium that David Layne had taken on as a business.

Jack represented the next stage of football coaching. The majority of managers and coaches up until the late 1950s were very stolid and staid, and hadn't got much more in their coaching arsenal apart from the desire to see the ball in the net. There was nothing as regards to how and where the ball should be kicked, or how players would link up to develop play. At many clubs, there wasn't even an opportunity to play with the ball. 'Keep the ball away from them during the week,' their thinking went, 'because then they'll be eager to have it on Saturday.'

When you're a player, you know straight away whether a coach has got the right attributes. Jack had the enthusiasm, information, and just the right amount of sarcasm to keep the players in check. If any of them started to get a bit 'big headed,' he would call them up on it. Some would get stroppy, but if they gave him a hard time, he would get on their back. He was a big inspiration for me throughout my coaching career. For me, that was the yardstick. If you could keep the players disciplined, you could coach them. For someone like Alan Finney, the very idea that Vic would bring a sackful of balls onto the training pitch was a revelation.

Gordon Clark's role was more ambiguous. He was of the old type, a solid man whose main function was to sweep up all the disorder that Vic left in his wake. Every so often, Vic would let him take a warm-up session. His pet thing was stretching exercises. He used to take us onto the terraces and tell us to prop one of our legs up on the terrace barriers, and then pull our heads down to our knees. I grew to detest them after I pulled a muscle in a continental game. I was sprinting down the wing when I suddenly felt a pain in my leg. It felt like someone had stuck a knife in the back of my thigh. The muscle developed scar tissue, and prevented it from stretching properly.

From then on, whenever I did stretching exercises, my muscle would tighten up and prevent me from going flat out for matches. One day, I decided that I'd had enough and confronted him. 'Gordon, every time I do your stretches, I feel awful on match days.' We reached a compromise. I would do the drills, but would only stretch as far as I felt comfortable with. I'd go through the motions of putting my leg up on the top of the terrace, but when I was supposed to put my head down, I would just nod it forward slightly.

*****

The next season didn't get off to the best of starts but in October we had the honour of playing Santos of Brazil, another Eric Taylor initiative. Santos had travelled the world making money from testimonial games and continental cups, and Eric found out that they had a game scheduled in Germany. It transpired that they had two days free so he persuaded them to make a flying visit to Sheffield. They played in Germany, then against us, and flew back. Nearly 50,000 people packed into Hillsborough.

When I caught sight of Pele for the first time, it was like seeing a little boy and I wasn't so scared. Once on the pitch I saw him come alive. Even though he didn't really fire that night I was amazed at how strong he was. Tony Kay jumped up on his back at one point to stop him, and Pele managed to run for about fifteen yards with him on his back. Peter Swan wanted his shirt and wouldn't let him out of his sight, so I decided I was going to get one as well. I set my sights on Dalmo, their number three.

We held our own, but were two-nil down after half an hour. After two minutes Pagao sent a forty yard pass over Peter Swan's head, and Coutinho swept it into the net. The second goal was more my fault. I was chasing Pele but he beat me to the ball and sent it in to Coutinho who scored. Billy Griffin and David Layne got us back level from Eddie Holiday crosses. We thought we could go in at half time level, but Coutinho waded through our entire defence and slipped the ball past Ron Springett, and then Tony Kay brought down Pele in the penalty box. Pele put the ball down on the penalty spot, took a few steps back, and then casually walked up to it, dummied, watched Ron dive one way, then rolled it into the other side of the net. I'd never seen anyone take a penalty like that before. Soon after, we got a penalty, and Colin Dobson tried to do the same. The Santos keeper didn't buy the dummy and just picked up Colin's shot.

A couple of weeks later we played Aston Villa at Hillsborough. It was the only time I was ever booed by Wednesday fans. Villa had a hard looking little nut called Jimmy MacEwan, and I was standing with him on the post defending a corner. The ball came in and I heard an 'Ugh.' I looked down at Jimmy and he was in a state, shaking, blood coming from his mouth, and some of his teeth missing. I looked around. All the Aston Villa players pointed at David Layne, who was protesting his innocence to the referee.

The referee consulted with the linesman and as neither had seen anything, they had no choice but to restart the game. Vic Crowe, the Villa captain, noticed soon after that David's hand had blood splattered on it. David made up a story but the referee decided that it was enough proof to send him off. The crowd however, seemed convinced that it was me who had knocked out Jimmy, and started booing every time I was on the ball. It was only after the match when I asked the guy who was in charge of the score board, that I found out that crowd thought I'd let David take the rap.

*****

The winter of 1962 was particularly harsh with huge amounts of snowfall across the whole of Britain. It was dangerous sometimes, because footprints from previous games would still be frozen onto the pitch come the next game. After playing Burnley on December 29th we had to wait until January 12th to play our next game against West Brom, and it was almost two months after that when we played Nottingham Forest on March 2nd.

We went into the Christmas period on a low. Tony Kay, who'd long been linked to other clubs, decided that he wanted to hook up with Harry Catterick at Everton. The fee, £55,000, was a British record for a wing half. Tony was a real original. He had the energy and the flamboyance that pushed us forward, and was always screaming and shouting and generally taking the mickey out of everyone. We were down at Owlerton one time and he was ribbing Gerry Young. Eventually, Jack Mansell intervened and told Tony to leave him alone. Tony responded, 'Referees never stopped me abusing team-mates.'

'I'm not the referee, I'm the coach!' Jack replied.

'You could have fooled me!' Tony shouted back. Jack took offence to this, pulled him out of the training match, and replaced him with Wilf Smith. That's how Tony was. Cocky, a joker, but always fiery. His departure gave Peter Eustace his chance in the first team. Peter was from Stocksbridge and very much lived up to the stereotypes of country living. He was a tweed wearer and into his shooting, and before he settled down with his wife, he was a bit of a man about town.

Once married though, Peter settled down into the routine of joining Yvonne and I for drinks. As a player at that time, our social lives revolved around the club. All of the players used to socialise with each other. It was such a great atmosphere to be playing with some of your best friends.

Peter wasn't in the team for all that long before he was replaced by Gerry Young, who finally got a game in his favoured position. Gerry was a quiet man, and good looking, apart from his nose which he had broken in the past and was bent to one side. He looked like a boxer who had taken one too many punches, but he wasn't the type of man to get it fixed. He was a friend to everyone, did his job, and then went home to his wife Beryl. He had an absolutely brilliant fake movement to go past people. I had seen it many times before it made its way into the first team.

Middlewood was out of action throughout the freeze, so we trained at the University of Sheffield Goodwin Sports Centre. Driving there one day, Keith Ellis and Vic had an argument. They were talking when suddenly Vic stated that all professional footballers were thick. Keith took exception to this, accusing Vic of being toffee-nosed. That really spelled the end for Keith. He'd already handed in a transfer request before, and with all the persistent talk that we were still after Joe Baker, I guess he got fed up of never being the first choice. As for Vic, well he always had a high assessment of his own opinions. He thought he was the authority on everything.

We couldn't do proper circuits in the gym, so Johnny Logan made us run in a figure of eight formation. One day, there was an electrician working on the lights and they had lifted up one of the floor boards to get to the well. We were flying around as fast as we could, and Johnny was backing up shouting, 'Come on. Give it everything you've got. Come on. Go the extra mile.' All of a sudden he disappeared. One minute we'd been looking at him telling us to sprint, and the next he'd gone. He'd only gone and backed up into the hole and fallen down it.

Due to the backlog of games, we ended up playing eight games in April. Fitness more often than not meant the ability to slog through pitches and survive. I don't think I ever saw a pitch inspection that called a game off for a waterlogged pitch, and I saw pitches with so much water on them that the ball pulled up after about ten yards. Teams like Manchester United, who liked to pass the ball, never liked coming to Hillsborough because it was always a quagmire. We were used to it, so it was a little bit easier for us.

We won five of our last six games to cement another sixth place finish, and played some great football, but the league wasn't as close – we finished thirteen points behind Everton. We began with a 2-0 victory at Anfield, one of the best performances we put in under Vic. Everything about our play that day oozed quality. I was involved in the second goal. Gerry Young slipped on the ball when passing it back to Ron Springett and Ian St. John, their hero, nipped in. He slipped it past Peter Swan to Roger Hunt, but I was able to get in the way at the very last moment and head the ball out to Peter Johnson, who booted it up field. The ball made its way to David Layne who hit it right across Tommy Lawrence into the corner of the net from a tight angle.

On May Day we visited Old Trafford. United were in the FA Cup Final but were deep in a relegation crisis and we did them 3-1. Alan got the first from a Colin Dobson cross that missed all their defenders. Five minutes later, he slipped the ball through to Johnny Quinn who got the second. The final goal was mine. We had a corner taken by Colin and as the ball was cleared away, I rushed forward from the middle of their half and hit it as hard as I could from thirty-five yards. It just flew. Even I was lost for words. I'd scored at Old Trafford. It took me a little while to come down after that.

6

Darlings of the West End

A lot has been made about the 1960-61 fight against Tottenham, but it wasn't an isolated moment of success. We went into the 1963-64 season on the back of four top six finishes, and though we'd lost Tony Kay and Bobby Craig, we still had the nucleus of a great side, with myself, Peter Swan, Gerry Young, and David Layne all entering our prime years.

The board, who were forever worrying about finances, knew that we needed another good season to keep the momentum going. Despite our high positions in the table, the results had never been quite as good as that last season under Harry Catterick, and the newspapers were full of articles about how Wednesday might need to sell players to stay out of debt if the home gates didn't increase. Being ambitious, the board wanted Wednesday to win the title, get European qualification, and carry on playing attractive football.

There was plenty of speculation over the summer that Vic might leave the club and return to Holland, first to Feyenoord, and then back to Ajax. This was followed in July by the explosion of the betting scandal. Though it had long been suspected that there was a large and influential betting ring, nothing substantial had come of it due to lack of evidence. Alan Hardaker, the FA Secretary, had been doing independent investigations but hadn't come up with much.

Then *The People* newspaper started to make its revelations. Esmond Million, the Bristol Rovers goalkeeper, was uncovered as having swung a home game against Bradford. The next week they announced that Million's go-between had been Brian Phillips, a centre half at Mansfield. He, Million, and Rovers striker Keith Williams, were all banned *sine die* from football for match fixing. In the course of the inquiries, Phillips made allegations that a Wednesday player was involved in illegal betting. Eric Taylor denied the allegations.

The 1963-64 season was our poorest start for six years. We were hindered by two major upheavals. Early on, Vic fell out with Jack Mansell, demoted him to reserve team coach, and put himself in charge of first team training. The tension between them often bubbled over into the dressing room. Vic would be doing a team talk and Jack would be in the corner of the room criticising him underneath his breath and quietly mouthing 'What the hell does he think he's talking about.'

Vic truly was a one-off, and that was perhaps his problem. He was supremely confident in his own abilities and fancied himself as the gentleman of soccer. Sometimes he'd start to talk, and he'd become so enraptured with what he was saying that he'd go into a trance. His hands would start to move, he'd walk around the room, and that would be that. Being such a raconteur, he'd become so involved in what he was saying that even if people walked away from him he'd just carry on talking. Like many people, Jack got weary of the act.

It was partly justified. Vic had his own style, and it probably wasn't the best way to communicate. I remember on one occasion he was trying to explain his continental approach to us in the dressing room. For some reason he had a golf club with him and was swinging it about him as if he was on the driving range. 'What we are not doing that I'd like you to do,' he said, 'is to change the pace at which we play. We need to slow the ball down, and then we need to make it go fast again. We've got Alan Finney on one wing and we've got Colin Dobson on the other. We will be going slow, quick, and then we'll knock it out wide, and Colin Dobson will go du du du du du du.'

What he meant was that he wanted us to be able to take it nice and easy and then press when we got into the danger zones.

This was fine for players who were comfortable on the ball, but for players like me it was a challenge to play skilfully at great speed. I wasn't always able to pick out passes immediately when I received the ball. Under pressure, I might not know who to pass to, or whether I should take the ball on a run. If I felt uncomfortable with the ball at my feet I wouldn't take a chance and turn around and play it short, I would hit it up field. I remember Peter Eustace used to tell me, 'Meggy. Put your foot on it and stop booting it.'

That's not to say we didn't like Vic. As he settled into the role, we grew to appreciate the perks of his style. He was exciting and fun, particularly when we travelled away from Sheffield. Eric Taylor had always gone to great lengths to try and prove that Wednesday were a better club than Sheffield United. Everything about us had to be that little bit classier. Nowhere was this better shown than when we used to travel to London for away games. Taylor knew that Sheffield United used to travel down on the morning of the match, and travel back later the same day, and so he believed that we had to do something different. He decided that Wednesday would travel down on the train the afternoon before, book into the Grosvenor Hotel, and take in a West End show on the evening.

In the West End, Vic really came alive. He lived and breathed the theatre, and loved to be associated with the big stars, several of whom he knew. We went with him to see the big shows of the day. *My Fair Lady*, *The Mouse Trap*, *How to Succeed in Business without Really Trying*, *Charlie Girls*. We saw them all. Or we might go to a concert, perhaps Cilla Black or Ken Dodd. One time, after seeing the Black and White Minstrel Show, we were invited down to the changing rooms to meet the stars of the show. On this occasion, Leslie Crowther was there. He and the other actors were taking off their make-up and Vic was going around kissing them, being the bon vivant. This used to perturb some of the players a little bit, as they saw his behaviour a little too exuberant.

We also visited some of London's most famous nightclubs, such as The Raymond Revue Bar in Soho, which could be considered a classy place in its heyday. It was a popular haunt for celebrities such as Peter Sellers, John Mills, Alma Cogan, and big American stars such as Judy Garland and Frank Sinatra. Most nights there would be a jazz band playing and there'd be a sing-along. One night we were sat around the stage watching a woman do a reverse strip routine. She started in a bubble bath covered in bubbles, and ended by walking off the stage in a two piece suit. She got out of the bath and there were bubbles everywhere. She flicked them into the audience with her fingers and somehow, a huge pile of them came loose and landed on Derek Wilkinson's face.

*****

Our injuries that year were horrendous. Of the first team squad, only Gerry Young and I managed to last the whole season. Peter Johnson only played ten games, pretty much surrendering his first team place to Brian Hill. After John Fantham was injured in October, there was much despair over how to replace him. Gates were still down, and the consensus on the board was that only a larger-than-life centre forward could pick things up. In the end it was Mark Pearson of Manchester United who fitted the bill.

Mark was an odd case. He came to us with a bad boy image, but I always knew him as a quiet lad. He'd come in every morning, put his coat on his peg, read his paper, and that was it. The likes of Eddie Holliday would come in and want to be the centre of attention, but Mark's ambitions lay elsewhere. I once asked him what he wanted to do after he retired as I was already thinking of going into coaching. He looked at me and said, 'All I want to do is go back to the village I'm from, go to the pub and have a pint with my dad.' That was Mark in a nutshell. You could see the skill but football didn't turn him on.

Mark arrived just in time for our Fairs Cup match against Cologne. In the first round we'd played DOS Utrecht, an amateur team who treated our participation as a big deal. The day before the first leg in Utrecht, we were taken to a Military Tattoo in our honour. I remember them walking onto the lush pitch at one end, and exiting a quagmire at the other end. The match itself was all ours. Eddie Holliday put us ahead after five minutes and it ended 4-1. It was the same score in the return leg. David Layne scored a hat trick in front of the Wednesday fans, before being taken to hospital with a dislocated shoulder after a heavy tackle. Colin Dobson got the other.

Cologne were more illustrious opponents. They were the top team in Germany that season and went on to win the league. Their stadium was a real tidy affair, with telegraph pole style floodlights and a mock castle house by the entrance, where the stadium administrator lived. We were picked up from the airport and driven to the stadium, where we were told under no circumstances were we able to practice on the pitch, so we had to hunt across town to find somewhere to train. I think we ended up training in a park.

As we walked onto the pitch we saw large groups of away fans waving white flags. The performance didn't quite match up to their efforts though. By half time we were 3-0 down. Wolfgang Overath was running the show, knocking balls out to the wingers all night long. But in the last ten minutes we managed to get back in it with two great finishes from Mark Pearson. The first came after he managed to weave his way through the entire Cologne defence, and the second came from a corner when Anton Schumacher was unable to keep out Mark's swerving shot.

Back at Hillsborough we were expected to perform well after a great win against Wolves a few days earlier, but we lost 2-1 after going ahead through a David Layne goal. I blamed myself for the defeat. Though their winger, Karl-Heinz Thelen, wasn't a good dribbler he was a powerful runner. I was marking him, but because we were ahead I'd decided to go on a forward overlap run and left him behind me. We lost possession and from there, they knocked the ball to him. He went on the run, swerved past Peter Swan, and placed the ball past Ron. Overath scored the second, jinking his way through the defence to slot home. That was the end of our European adventure.

With Mark's influence however, we climbed to fourth over Christmas, beating Bolton Wanderers 3-0 at Hillsborough on

Christmas Eve. It set us in a good mood for the club party, which that year was held at the Beehive Pub. Alan Finney, who liked to have fun, decided that instead of going straight home to Doncaster he'd come back to mine for a nightcap. I didn't live all that far from Hillsborough so it seemed like a good idea.

Instead of having a coffee and letting a little bit of time go, Alan had a couple of whiskeys. When he left, I watched him up the road in his Volkswagen and everything seemed fine. When he reached Holme Lane however, he hit a parked car with such force that one of his wing mirrors fell off. Because he was a little drunk, he set off and left it behind, not realising until he'd got home.

What he didn't know was that a man had retrieved the wing miror, taken down his car number, and reported it to the police, who then contacted Alan to warn him that he was liable for the damage. The next home game a man walked up to him and told Finn he was sorry he had told the police but he didn't know it was him. Alan cursed, 'You bloody nutter.' I can't remember what happened after that, but I picked up the newspaper that evening and the headline was 'The Winger Who Lost His Wing.'

Before the end of the season, Eddie Holliday and Colin Dobson would also get in trouble for driving offences. Eddie was found slumped over the wheel of his car drunk, while Colin ran a few red lights. This inevitably drew criticism from the board who accused Vic of letting discipline slide. Also around that time, Peter Johnson wrote a letter to the board stating all the things that he thought Buckingham was at fault for.

*****

For our first game of 1964 we travelled to Wales for an FA Cup third round tie against Fourth Division Newport County. The Newport ground was a sight to behold, it really was out of another age. The dressing room was tiny, and for whatever reason, the baths were in an adjacent crawl space, and only accessible by climbing through an exposed brick wall.

It was the worst Wednesday performance I'd encountered up to that point. Every time Brian Hill or myself cleared the ball, it came straight back at us. We went in at half time 1-0 up without deserving it. After the break they equalised, which prompted a pitch invasion, and the game was halted. When it resumed, we were even more off our kilter and they went ahead. Alan Finney equalised and it looked to be ending 2-2 until Roy McLaren, who was in goal that day, caught a ball from a punt downfield. One of their players came in to shoulder barge him after he caught it, and it made him lose his concentration. He cleared the ball straight to their striker who shot it straight back past him.

The worst part of the day came after the match was over. After we'd bathed and got changed, we got on the coach, which dropped us off at Newport Station. It was there that we realised that we'd be making our way back to Sheffield on the supporters train!

Going into the second half of the season, all of the teams that were above us had to play at Hillsborough, and we needed to get into a good run of form. We looked to have got things back on track the following week when we beat Ipswich 4-1 away and Sheffield United 3-0 at Hillsborough. And for a moment, we thought we might push on and get the top spot. But in the next home game we crumbled to a 3-0 defeat to Everton. That was the moment when it started to come undone for Vic.

Ron was suffering from a stressful year. He'd been dropped from the England squad, and was injured in our next game against West Brom. He was out for eight weeks, and when he came back he was dropped for the home game against Arsenal in favour of Roy McLaren. Roy was a reasonable goalkeeper, but it wasn't the same as having the England number one behind you. Vic didn't seem to have any one solution to the problem. He would spend hours agonising in his office over who to play and what the best formation would be. When it worked, it worked, but when it failed, he'd immediately go back to the drawing board instead of sticking with something.

Like Harry before him, Vic started to become aggrieved at the fact Ron lived in London. Ron was affronted at being dropped, after all he had more caps as a goalkeeper than any previous international player, and he thought he deserved to be first choice when fit so he decided to hand in a transfer request. In an effort to resolve the matter, the club called a meeting of all the directors, to which Ron brought a handful of grievances he had against Vic. His transfer request was rejected by the board.

Days later, Gordon Clark left to manage Peterborough, and the writing seemed on the wall. The next week, Vic was told that his contract would not be extended past the end of the season. Just like Harry Catterick had found, if you went against Ron Springett you went against Eric Taylor.

*****

Sunday April 12th, 1964 was planned as a quiet day for me, relaxing with the family. But at 9:00am I heard some hustle and bustle from outside. I went to the bedroom window and looked outside. I saw a circus of *People* reporters coming down the street to knock on Peter's door. The match fixing scandal had come to the First Division. Peter Swan, Tony Kay and David Layne had placed bets against Wednesday in a game at Ipswich in the 1962-63 season. My initial thoughts were of dumbfoundment. 'Clowns, what were they doing?'

I think that I speak for most of the players in saying that we felt an amount of sympathy for the three, because they were treated harshly compared to other players who were caught in the sting. I think the only person who didn't have any sympathy for them was Vic. 'Don't feel sorry for them,' he told us in the dressing room. 'They might as well have just walked into the dressing room when you weren't there and pinched your four pound match bonus from out of your coat pocket.'

All of the first team squad were taken in for questioning by the police. Peter Johnson and Alan Finney in particular were interrogated at length, because they were known to enjoy gambling on fixed odds, which was allowed back then. Peter had played really poorly at Ipswich against their winger Jimmy Leadbetter, and had been given four out of ten in *The People*. The police wanted to know why he had played so poorly, and he got irate with them saying 'Anyone can have a bad game.'

Then it was my turn. They asked me my name and profession

and whether I liked to place bets. I told them no, I wasn't much of a betting man. Then they asked me about the game. I couldn't remember that much, it had been a fairly unremarkable game. I vaguely remembered that Peter hadn't headed as many balls as he usually did. David had got steamrolled by Vic at half time because he was spending too much time out wide, but played well throughout the second half. Tony Kay had been the star man that day.

We were due to play at Hillsborough on the Monday in a re-arranged fixture against Tottenham, because a number of the players had been involved in an England v. Scotland international on the Saturday. The FA had suspended Peter and David, so Derek Wilkinson and Vic Mobley started in their place. At half time, Eric Taylor gave a speech informing the crowd to stick with the club through the challenging period. We won the game 2-0 with both goals from Derek. Funnily enough, it was our second highest attendance of the season.

We finished off the season with an away draw at Blackpool, ensuring another sixth place finish. Again, we'd finished eight points off the title winners, but Liverpool were no Tottenham double-winning side. Given the number of injuries we'd had throughout the season we were probably a little bit unlucky, but our inconsistency let us down. When we looked at the results, we saw a whole lot of matches that we should and could have won, and wondered if it may have been different if we'd all been fit. It was the last hurrah for the players who'd formed the core of the 1958-59 promotion team. Over the following two years the team changed drastically, as did the atmosphere around the club. Certainly, the scandal cast a shadow, one that took a long time for the club to emerge from.

7

Chasing Shadows

If you wanted to get yourself out of Hillsborough during the mid-1960s, then challenging Alan Brown was the quickest way to find the exit. For four years, he ruled over Hillsborough with an iron fist – it was his way, or the highway. As a stern coach who thrived on discipline, many journalists viewed his appointment as the statement of a new era at Wednesday, and an attempt to draw a line over the embarrassment that the club had faced over the betting scandal.

I'd first met Alan in 1953. I was supposed to be playing in Nottingham with the youth team but had arrived late at Hillsborough. At the time, Alan Brown was working at the club as a coach under Eric Taylor, and as I walked into the front office at Hillsborough he walked up and told me that I'd missed the coach. 'Will you be able to get him to Nottingham?' he asked my dad.

So I got back in my dad's car and drove down to Nottingham as fast as we could. Alan, to his credit, phoned ahead to warn them that we would be arriving. Luckily, the coach had stopped off for lunch, so we ended up getting there before the team.

In 1954 Alan departed to manage Burnley, where he set up their training centre, going as far as to help build it, and also persuaded the Chairman to let him strengthen the club's youth set up. Three years later, he moved to crisis club Sunderland where his integrity helped the club recover from a series of scandals about illegal payments to players. It was after Vic left, that he made his move back to Wednesday.

My first opportunity to get to know Alan came on a tour to Germany in the summer of 1964. It was a trip to forget. From the moment Alan walked into the dressing room for the first time, he clashed with the players who had strong personalities, and in particular Peter Johnson. As an Alan Brown player, you had to fully accept that he wouldn't tell you something if he didn't believe that it was the best course of action for you and the club. If you fought back, you were gone.

I knew that stern words had been shared behind the scenes, and there was a tense feeling in the dressing room whenever Peter and Alan spoke to each other. Peter essentially told Alan that he was wrong with some of the decisions he was making as coach. Alan turned around and stated: 'I'm the manager, I can never be wrong!'

'You're not God.' Peter shouted.

That was that. It didn't matter to Alan that Peter had given eight years of service, or that I had a great understanding with him on the pitch. Peter had crossed Alan, and that was more than enough reason for him to be frozen out. He only played a couple of games after that and spent most of the time as the twelfth man in training exercises.

Everything about Alan was power, discipline, and moral fortitude. During his time at Sunderland he'd joined the Moral Re-Armament movement. Before that he'd swore and generally been a bit of a jack-the-lad, but one day he gathered all of his players into the dressing room, and with his wife present in the room with them, confessed all his failings, including a couple of affairs. Not that he ever mentioned Jesus or religion to us. He'd just explode at anything that he perceived as an injustice, or inappropriate behaviour.

Back at the airport we were going through customs. I'd bought a German watch and decided to go through without declaring it. Once we got to the other side, Alan overheard me telling some of the others what I'd done. He pulled me to one side and said, 'Is that true Don? Did you not declare that watch?' He'd told me that I'd let myself down morally and that I should have declared it. Of course, I didn't really see it as anything, but to him, I had been deliberately untruthful.

Eddie Holliday and Mark Pearson were late for the plane, and were only just coming through customs when it was time to board. The flight crew were more than willing to wait for them to arrive, but after five minutes, Alan got up out of his chair, stormed to the cockpit and shouted to the crew: 'Come on, just go!'

'We can't go Mr Brown. We're waiting on two passengers.'

Alan screamed at the top of voice. 'GET THIS PLANE OFF THE TARMAC!' We left Eddie and Mark in Amsterdam. Alan was obviously determined to give us all a lesson in timekeeping and discipline but unfortunately for him, the two were both able to catch another plane and managed to get back to Hillsborough before us. He was not pleased.

That's not to paint Alan as an ogre. David Ford, who was only eighteen at the time, had broken his leg during his début against Werder Bremen. Alan had carried him up the steps of the plane to get home, carried him down them when we touched down in Manchester, and drove him to Park Hill where he lived. If you were with Alan, he was with you all the way.

Tom McAnearney was the next to go. Alan had held Tom up to the younger players as an example of a good professional, but Tom also disagreed with Alan's methods. At the end of September we travelled to Denmark to play a friendly against AGF Aarhus. We lost the game 4-1 and played terribly. Nothing seemed to be going right, particularly for Colin Dobson. As we came off the pitch at half time, Alan grabbed hold of Colin and marched him into the toilets for a 'debrief.' When they returned, Colin was as white as a sheet.

While Alan was absolutely fuming, going at us with this and that, an old man with glasses half way down his nose, wandered into the dressing room with a tray of oranges. He placed them down on the corner table and then slowly ambled back up the corridor. A moment later, Alan marched over to the table without breaking his sentence, grabbed hold of the tray, and threw it all the way up the corridor. We were trying very hard not to laugh.

Then Tom lost himself and answered back. Oddly, Alan didn't explode. He simply picked up a football, and threw it at me. He pointed at Tom, 'You're not going out in the second half.' He pointed at me, 'You're going to be captain.' Tom was subbed for Peter Eustace. Tom and Alan never spoke again and Tom wasn't even given a testimonial, even though he'd given fifteen years service to the club.

As we ran on to the pitch for the second half, Colin mentioned to David Smith, one of Alan's coaches, 'Thank god I'm on the wing. It's the furthest point from the dug-out in the second half! At least I can avoid Alan.' Unfortunately for Colin, Alan spent the second half sat in the stand on Colin's side of the pitch shouting at him. The Danish fans must have wondered what was going on.

My first full game as captain came the following week. From Aarhus we travelled to Düsseldorf to play a National Select Eleven in the Rhine Stadium. It was the first game of Germany's build up to the 1966 World Cup, and they took it very seriously by fielding seven internationals including Uwe Seeler, and Wolfgang Overath. Gerry Young played particularly well, and soon after we returned home, he received a call-up to the national squad for a game against Wales.

Gerry was really unlucky. He'd pulled his leg on the tour but really wanted to play in the match as he didn't know if it would be his only chance to play for England. With England, players get judged on what people see, not on how the player feels. If he'd sat out until he was fit, he might have established himself. On the other hand, he might never have got called up again. He ended up playing and unfortunately aggravated his leg to such an extent that he was out for most of the season.

I never doubted that I had the necessary qualities to be a captain. Alan often took me to one side to discuss his intentions and the general tactics and shape of the side, as well as other things that the rest of the team wouldn't know. We had an arrangement where if I thought something on the pitch wasn't working, I had Alan's consent to change things around, as long as I could justify the changes to him after the game. So if I saw a player flying up the field too much instead of sitting back and holding the ball, I had Alan's blessing to go up to him, remind him of his responsibilities, and if necessary change the situation to our advantage.

I absolutely loved coming out to play for Wednesday, and I really did genuinely play for the fans. And I always tried to give everything that I had, and told the younger players the same. 'Don't cheat them. Show the crowd that you'll give everything. If you do, they will respond.' Within the club, Derek Dooley was a big champion of me, and thought I was the best full back he'd ever seen.

*****

That season, Wednesday agreed a deal with Newton Chambers to rent Thorncliffe Sports Ground at Chapeltown for training purposes. It was the first time that Wednesday had ever made use of a dedicated facility and Alan ensured that we made more than full use of it. Training under him was intense, organised and repetitive. His crusade was shadow play, which ruled over everything we did.

We'd arrive at Thorncliffe and before training started, we'd play table tennis and generally have a laugh. Then Alan would arrive. We'd put on our training kit and for half an hour he'd let us do what we wanted, whilst he sat in the club house. The wingers would be knocking balls in for headers, someone would get a ball and put in a shot. I eventually realised that this was deliberate. Though it looked like free time, it was controlled. It was Alan's way of letting us have a little bit of fun together.

Then he would come out and the shadow play would start. Essentially, we were playing against nothing. Three or four players would take on the role of defenders, and each would have a player to mark. We would be working out a routine and all of a sudden Alan would shout, 'Free kick against you.' We'd all know exactly where to go to get into the places that we should be in if a free kick was being taken from that position. You'd sprint to get the wall together, and then make sure you were in the correct place. The exact opposite would work up the other end. We'd be pushing forward against nothing and he would shout, 'Free kick forward.'

One of our free kick routines was for the taker to line up the shot while I stood behind them on the wing pretending to fiddle with my shoe laces, watching the wall to see if they were paying any notice. At the very last second I would sprint down the side of the wall to collect the ball and then hit it across the six-yard box, knowing full well that one of the other players would be coming in to get it.

It was football tactics to the nth degree, with nothing left to chance. 'Stop there,' he'd say. 'You see this? This is what I want from this position. This is how you play a one-two. You do that. You get over here, you get over there.

'David Ford, you come on a run from inside to outside.

'Don, you get hold of it and float it over the full back. Throw in there.'

When Jimmy McCalliog first arrived at the club, I used to fall out with him over these tactics. 'Can we not just play a bit of five-a-side?' he used to ask. He and the other young players wanted to have a giggle and a friendly kick about. Because Alan had told me to miss out the midfield in my passing, Jimmy would often come forward and indicate for me to pass to him. I would ignore him. I'd tell him, 'Jim, it's about drawing the player out with you, so I can hit it into the space behind for you to spin round and collect. Don't expect the ball to your feet.'

Alan's original coaching team consisted of Ian MacFarlane and David Smith. Ian had worked with Alan at Sunderland, while David had been a protégé of Alan's at Burnley, and joined Wednesday after a period spent coaching in Libya. His brief was to develop the youth players. In my opinion, he was treated badly by Alan. He was a professional coach, yet Alan treated him like an apprentice, giving him odd jobs like cleaning boots and packing skips.

It got to the stage where David wasn't doing any of the coaching at all. One time we were training and Dave was walking past us with a big bag of footballs slung over his shoulders. Alan had told him to bring the balls, which David did. He walked to the front, placed the balls beside him, and Alan clapped his hands: 'RIGHT! We're finished. Go inside.' And David had to pick up the balls and carry them back inside. I thought to myself, 'That isn't on.'

There was a glut of promising young players starting to come up through the ranks into the reserve side that first year with Alan. The best of the bunch was John Hickton. He was the only player I ever played with who I thought was too good for me. He was strong, could score goals, and he was a good tackler. Derek Dooley had marked him out as his successor, and Alan had taken him under his wing just as he had with Derek a decade earlier. He'd started off as a centre half in the reserves, but it quickly became apparent that he had an eye for goal. I would come into the ground on a morning and be told that the Reserves had won 5-4 and John had scored three from defence.

Andy Burgin was another player I took an interest in. He only played three games in the first team, and made his début against Everton in the FA Cup third round in January 1965 because Brian Hill was injured. On the team bus driving to Liverpool I gave him little pieces of joking advice, to get him revved up for the game. 'If you make any mistakes,' I told him, 'blame someone else.' We were halfway through the first half and it was 0-0. Suddenly, an Everton player played a good through ball and Andy sliced it into our net. He turned to me and asked who to blame for that.

Late into the season Alan Finney was injured quite badly at Burnley. He'd never really got on with Alan Brown, even back to the days when he was a young player and Alan was a coach at the club. Alan believed he was being ignored because he was over thirty. After the injury he only played about five more matches and didn't make the Cup Final team. He was sold to Doncaster rather than being allowed to leave on a free transfer, which would have got him more money.

We were upset because the next year, his testimonial was held on the same day that we were coming back from Wembley. He'd been promised a high profile match against Sheffield United at Hillsborough, but had nothing in writing. Wednesday wouldn't allow it to be held at Hillsborough because of the World Cup matches that were going to be played there. It also meant that if we won the Cup, we wouldn't be able to parade it in front of the fans. We ended up playing the game in Doncaster.

We reflected on this and other things during the end of season tour, which took on a spontaneous flavour. We weren't that happy when we went behind the Iron Curtain because it was never that welcoming, but Krakow was a beautiful city, as was Katowice, which had many Art Nouveau buildings, where we played a Polish Combination XI.

When I went on tours I always used to buy things that the country was famous for. Katowice was known for its crystal glass so I bought an expensive vase and had it wrapped up. After the match we went on a trip to Auschwitz, the very definition of depression. On the way we'd been telling jokes, which was usual for a tour. But when we went through the famous gates an eerie silence descended, which continued as we went through all the rooms, viewing the hair, shoes, cases, and thousands of spectacles, and then into the gas chambers. We came out and the feeling was uniformly morose. We got back on the coach and the enormity of it all hit us. It was the saddest feeling you could ever experience

On returning to the airport for the flight home, Eric got us together and told us all to phone our wives and girlfriends. There'd been a change of plan. Instead of flying home straight away, we were going to fly to Spain and play a match against Valencia. Once we got there, we drove through the countryside for about two hours and when we arrived, the place was absolutely bursting. There were women screaming as if the Beatles were there. At first we thought it might be because of us, but in fact they were there for El Cordobes, the most famous bullfighter in Spain at the time.

We booked into the hotel, only to find that the match wasn't starting until midnight. Alan Finney and Derek Wilkinson decided to walk into the El Cordobes reception, and ended up being invited to the fight by the man himself. I asked Alan Brown if we could go and watch the bullfights. He said no, on account of not wanting us to be out in the sun all afternoon. It might not have been ideal preparation because Valencia was a good side and we lost 3-0.

The next day, we arrived at the airport thinking that we were now going to fly home. But once again we were told by Eric and Alan that we weren't. While we'd been playing Valencia, Eric Taylor had been on the phone arranging a match in Ireland against Shamrock Rovers. All through the journey, I was looking after my crystal glass vase.

When most people go away on holiday and have to stand waiting in the airport, they usually just put their bags around them. But when it came to Wednesday tours, Alan thought this was untidy. He wanted us to place all our belongings in a long line. On this occasion we hadn't, and as soon as Alan noticed that he started throwing our bags across the airport corridor. He reached for my bag and I screamed, 'NO, THAT'S GLASS!' I stopped him just in time.

Shamrock Rovers were a better team than we thought, and we only just scraped through. We were pretty fatigued by that point, and a few of the players just wanted to get home. Graham Pugh, who was only nineteen at the time, wasn't really putting any effort in and as captain I decided to have a bit of a go at him.

'**** off,' he shouted back.

I was livid.

Graham was playing right half, so he wasn't that far from me and I started running towards him. He glanced at me in terror, turned right round, and ran off the pitch and up the tunnel. I caught up with him just shy of the changing room door and grabbed him by the shirt. 'If you ever tell me to **** off again, I'll deck you. Now get out there and put some effort in.'

Graham was a funny lad, who had his own sense of humour. I felt for him, because Wednesday ultimately let him down. He had an injured knee and Wednesday mis-diagnosed him. A piece of cartilage that he'd damaged had grown back and was left unnoticed. He put on a load of weight and was never able to shift it off.

8

The Road to Wembley

I don't think there's ever a time in a cup run where you think you can win it. And if you'd asked me at the beginning of the 1965-66 season whether we'd get to Wembley, I would have probably laughed at you, because it was far from a glorious season. But with results in the league taking us nowhere near to the heights of previous years, with each round that went by we started to think that it might be our year. At that time, the draw was done from a bag with all the balls in it, with each ball being a team. Every round we went through, Vic Mobley would say, 'Let's keep the ball in the bag.' It became the call as we ran out of the dressing room for each game.

Alan was a fine manager, but the quality of players at his disposal was declining. Many of the experienced players who'd boosted the team were now gone. This was compounded by Alan's decision to follow the lead of England manager Alf Ramsey and dispense with wingers, and both Colin Dobson and new signing Brian Usher struggled to get in the side. Colin made the mistake of talking to one of the directors about possibly wanting a transfer, and when Alan found out what had happened he stormed into the dressing room, grabbed hold of Colin, and tried to hang him by his coat from one of the pegs. Though he continued to feature, Colin's performances declined and he left at the end of the season to join Huddersfield.

Our FA Cup journey began at Reading in the third round, and it was the closest we came to getting knocked out, with Jimmy

McCalliog scoring late to get us the win. Then we travelled to St James' Park, which was a hotbed of a place to play. The atmosphere that night was fantastic and we played really well. We'd practiced my free kick routine before the match and this time it worked a treat. The Newcastle defenders missed me going down the line and I whacked the ball in as hard as I could. It zipped across the six-yard box, hit John McGrath on the knee, and went in the net for an own goal.

The Huddersfield game in the fifth round was fairly pedestrian. Brian Usher scored the winner in awful conditions. Then Blackburn Rovers in the quarter-final. David Ford played really well and scored two great goals. At the time, Blackburn were still a great side. I marked Brian Douglas, and they also had Roy Vernon, Ronnie Clayton and Peter Dobing playing that day.

And then we met Chelsea at Villa Park. We knew that any result we got against them would be an upset, because they had eight internationals in their side. The most memorable thing about the game was the conditions. It had rained heavily the night before and the pitch was a sea of mud. As we stepped onto the playing surface we instinctively ran lightly to stop ourselves sinking into the mud. Villa's ground was being renovated and there was no dugout. I eyed Tommy Docherty, the Chelsea manager, sat on a temporary bench at far side of the pitch.

The surface suited us more than it did Chelsea, because we were stronger and more direct. We avoided playing back passes all game, because we didn't know if the ball would hold up in the mud. We got it up front as quickly as possible, and avoided laying balls to the midfielders. Chelsea on the other hand, were playing out to the full backs and building from there, but it wasn't working.

We set the tone from the start. The ball was knocked towards their left winger, Bobby Tambling, who was taken out by Wilf Smith with a really tough tackle. Right afterwards, I tackled his opposite number Bobby Bridges. We had them in our pockets from then on. But close to half time, Vic Mobley was clattered by George Graham, who gave him a hairline fracture in his ankle. I was annoyed by the tackle, and got even more incensed when I heard George shout, 'I've done him,' and I spent the rest of the game trying to get revenge on him.

Alan Brown liked to do all the important work himself. We had a physio called Bob Lyttle who strapped up Vic's ankle inside the boot, but Alan decided that he'd strap the outside of his boot as well. Vic got stuck up front, doing his best when he got a chance and hoping that he could get a knock-on. By the end of the game, his ankle had swollen up to such a state that he was unable to play in the final. We only found out that he had a fracture weeks later when, during the World Cup, we were able to use an X-Ray machine that had been brought over from Germany for their game against Switzerland at Hillsborough.

We got two late goals to win 2-0. Jimmy McCalliog scored one, and celebrated by doing a forward roll into a stretch of mud, while Graham Pugh got the other. His wasn't a spectacular goal. Vic Mobley got up for a header and knocked it across and Graham headed it in. As I left the pitch at the end of the game, I walked past Tommy Docherty who was making his way to the tunnel. He came striding up to me and shouted, 'You ****ing butcher, you don't deserve to be going to Wembley.' This from Tommy, who'd been known as a butcher for his entire career!

Then I was in the dressing room. It was an absolutely brilliant feeling. We were going to Wembley. Tony Hardisty came in to do the match report. 'I'm so proud of these lads,' I shouted. 'Six of them are youngsters. Whatever happens in the Final, we'll do a lap of honour at Wembley.'

There were about six games between the semi-final and the Final, and I don't think we won any of them. Alan had decided that he was going to chop and change the line up in order to keep the first team fresh, and it was difficult. Wednesday weren't really geared up to make that many changes and I think I was the only player who wasn't rested.

The run-up to the Final was less than smooth. It was common knowledge that when a team went to Wembley the players were given a stack of tickets apart from their official allocation. And though nobody ever said anything about it, it was common practice for players to sell on those tickets for more than face value. It was morally suspect, and of course Alan Brown wanted nothing to do with it. The players came to see me. 'Meg, we're not going to be getting our allocation of tickets, will you go and see what you can do to make sure that we get them?'

Being team captain, it was my responsibility to act on behalf of the team. I went to speak to Alan and asked him what was happening. I told him that all the team were disappointed that they wouldn't be getting the same allocation as Everton as we were only getting twelve. Alan looked at me and I knew instantly that it was a lost cause. 'Well, twelve is what you're allowed, so that's what you're going to get. No player of mine is going to be a scalper.'

I asked him why Everton were getting more tickets. 'Nothing to do with us,' he replied. He was convinced that the Everton players were not going to get anywhere near the amount of tickets that had been quoted. 'Well I know that because you've been in the game a long time, you could probably make use of 100 tickets, but Graham Pugh probably doesn't even know a hundred people. It's obvious that he's going to sell them on the black market. He will get his twelve tickets and that's that.'

A few days later I was sat in David Layne's café. The door opened, and three crombie-coated men walked in. They approached the man at the counter who nodded his head in my direction. All three of them came over to me. 'Can we have a word with you?' one of them asked, so I said no problem.

They sat down around me. Without speaking, one of them reached into his coat pocket and put a huge wad of money on the table. 'Right then, there's 4,000 quid there and we want all your tickets. No pissing around.'

'Eh. Hang on a second. I can't take that. I don't know how many tickets we are going to get. We have been told we are only going to get twelve.'

He replied, 'Don't be stupid. Everybody knows that you get 100. It's a well known fact.'

By this time, it had emerged that the Everton players had their tickets taken off them as a precaution. The London touts wanted our tickets and we hadn't even got them. I turned down the money and they left.

That weekend, we were playing Blackburn Rovers. We weren't that far from the ground when one of the players came up to me asking about his tickets. I got all the players together at the back of the coach and told them that we would only get twelve tickets each. They were incensed. Some of them told me that they would not play in the Final. 'We're not going to play. We're going to make a stand together so we can get our fair share of tickets.'

I told Alan what the players were feeling. All he said to me was, 'Right! Thanks for bringing that to my attention.'

After the game, the players were assembling in the dressing room when Alan came in. 'Right. I understand that some of you are not going to play at Wembley so let's have it right.' At that moment John Fantham walked into the dressing room from the bathroom. Alan pointed at him and shouted, 'Fantham, you will lose your shop. If you don't want to play, it's gone.' John, of course, was instantly on the back foot because he had never said anything about not playing.

Alan went on, 'I will play the reserves in the Cup Final. None of you are playing,' and then he marched out. He was quiet on the coach home, but the next thing we knew he had organised a press conference. He told the journalists that he'd rather quit than see us get an unfair ticket allocation. 'What am I running, a football team or a ticket agency?' It was understandable really. He'd worked very hard to get us to play well enough to be there, and he saw it as a personal betrayal that some of the players didn't appear to be as focused as he was.

One of the reporters at the press conference was a man called Frank McGee. I told him we were only going to get a small number of tickets and he arranged to come over from Manchester the next day and talk to me about it. The next day I told him the situation. 'That is absolutely ridiculous,' he said. 'They can't do that. And Alan says you won't play. That is ridiculous.' Then next morning I picked up the paper and the headline read – GREEDY WEDNESDAY PLAYERS. They bloody hammered us.

After training the next day, Alan took me to one side. 'You do know what I'm trying to do? This game is the most important match you'll ever play in your life. There's a medal at the end of the corridor and it's got your name on it. That's all that you should be thinking about, not tickets.'

Alan knew that I was representing the players, but he also knew that when it came to making a decision, if the players were faced with the prospect of not playing in the Cup Final they would fold, and I would stand alone. By that time a couple of the players had come up to me and said that they had never mentioned anything about not wanting to play. I called a team meeting in the players lounge. 'Okay,' I said. 'We aren't going to get the tickets. Who's for standing together to get more tickets?' Based on the reaction after the Blackburn game, I thought that the hands would go up again, but only about four went up.

Things came to a head soon after. Alan brought Ron Springett up from London on a weekday and called each player into his office one at a time and asked them if they were going to play. I'm not saying that if I'd gone in first I'd have said the same thing, but I went in last. He told me, 'You are the only one who is not going to play.' And I was, I stood alone. I mean, who in their right mind doesn't play in an FA Cup Final? Alan was a fair man though. A few days later, he told us that he'd arranged for us to get twelve tickets as members of the team, and twelve tickets in our family's name. We ended up getting twenty-four tickets. Alan would never break, not even if his life depended on it.

*****

The Final was the biggest moment of my career as like many players, I'd been steeped in the FA Cup from an early age. Even now, I think that most English players dream of playing in the FA Cup Final more than any other match. I'd played games for the FA, I'd played at all of the great First Division grounds, but never at Wembley. The week before the game and after the Final was like being a superstar. We were opening shops and were up on the balcony at the town hall, it was an unbelievable two weeks.

We went down to Lilleshall with Alan Brown for training the weekend before the Final. Johnny Logan and David Smith were left behind to pack the kit, and didn't join us until the day before the game. Right before the match, I gave my false teeth to Bob Lyttle, and impressed on him the importance of giving them back to me when I went up to get the trophy from Princess Margaret. I didn't want to walk up into the royal box with no teeth.

I never gave it a thought that we were playing against Harry Catterick. The only time I ever made a connection was when the ball landed with Alex Scott, who was quick and really hard to handle. But he made the mistake of waiting for it and I nailed him with a really hard, vicious tackle. It was a bad one because I whacked him up in the air and felt a little embarrassed afterwards. Tommy Eggleston came running on and called me a dirty bastard. 'Don't call me a dirty bastard' I shouted. 'It was you that used to encourage me to do that.'

We got off to a great start. One of our tricks at the time was that if we were in the right area when we were given a throw-in, we would throw it low and up the pitch alongside David Ford , allowing him to make a run forward. Peter Eustace threw it into David, who ran down the wing before knocking in a cross with his right foot from the left. Jimmy McCalliog got on the end of it and it was 1-0 after only four minutes.

After a quarter of an hour, I realised that my mouth had gone dry from nerves. David Smith was on sponge duties and had run onto the pitch to treat Wilf Smith. I saw this as an opportunity to get some water. I jogged over, picked up the sponge and sucked on it. It was brand new and tasted of rubber. I spat it out and said, 'Dave, what have you done with that?'

We went in at half time confident, and it was a fantastic goal that doubled our lead with half an hour left. John Fantham picked up the ball in the centre circle and shot off down the pitch on a sprinting run. He let off a shot which Gordon West could only parry, and David Ford hit in the rebound.

People have told me since that if it had stayed at 1-0 we would have kept our tails up and won the match. I don't know if they are right or not. The moment you go 2-0 up, the other team start to take up false positions as they press to get back into the game. A previously cautious player would have to attack more, and go gung ho in an effort to get a goal back.

Letting in the first goal is always an important turning point. I gave away a free kick that wasn't a foul, and Alex Scott hit in a cross. Brian Labone met the ball with a poor header, but somehow it ended up at the feet of Mike Trebilcock who half volleyed it into the net past six pairs of legs. I'd never heard of Mike before the match, and I never heard of him again after it.

The second goal was luck over judgement. Trebilcock got onto a headed ball in the box and again it landed great for him. To lose a 2-0 lead was a shattering experience, but once they'd equalised, we started to settle down a bit and work towards a third goal. We began to get back into the game.

Nothing could legislate for the third goal. The ball found its way to Tommy Wright, their right back, and he looked for a long pass up field that went to Gerry Young. Gerry hadn't put a foot wrong throughout the game, but momentarily lost a bit of concentration and the ball went under his foot. What could go wrong went wrong as the ball set up nicely for Derek Temple who was sprinting down the middle of the pitch even though he was a winger. He ran onto the ball and thundered a really good shot that left Ron with no chance.

Three goals in fourteen minutes and the match was lost 3-2. After the final whistle Ron Springett and I had our photographs taken on the pitch with our runner-up medals. Immediately after, the Wembley steward came over to us and pointed towards the dressing rooms, indicating that we had to leave so Everton could take to the field.

In all my years watching FA Cup Finals, I'd always thought it was sad to watch the players trudge off the field at the end, walking from the Royal Box straight to the changing rooms. But I had other plans. I'd told the players of my intention to do a lap of honour, and at that moment I set off looking for players. The first man I got to was Peter Eustace. 'Right Peter, don't let me run round this pitch on my own.' Soon enough, the entire team was with me and it was a proud moment. As we stood in the player's entrance with the stadium half empty, I told them, 'Don't worry, we'll be back.'

In the changing room the atmosphere was down and even Alan Brown was quiet. We'd all got in the bath, when Harry Catterick came in with the Cup and offered to let us drink from it, which was a nice gesture. But it was one that I was never going to accept. There was only one way I was ever going to drink from the FA Cup, and that was if I had won it.

I walked into my bedroom at the Grosvenor Hotel a couple of hours later, by which time the brave front had started to slip. The match was still fresh in my memory and I was absolutely distraught, reliving key moments in my mind, trying to decide whether I'd made the right decisions. Yvonne was preparing for the post match banquet and had no time to listen to me moaning about the things that we should've or shouldn't have done. 'You can't win them all Don. Somebody's got to lose.'

The next day we returned to Sheffield. The council had arranged an open top bus tour to take us round Sheffield on our return, and we all thought how embarrassing it would be if nobody turned up. I'd seen myself in my mind's eye walking around with a cup, exactly as I'd seen Ronnie Starling do after the 1935 Final. Thinking that we'd embarrassed ourselves, we came out of the station expecting a quiet reception.

The place was absolutely packed. We climbed onto the open top bus and started round the city centre. We didn't go any distance without people waving, and when we got to the City Hall, it was estimated that there were 200,000 people there. We were led in through a side door so we had no idea just how busy it was. We were taken up to the balcony and went outside. Barkers Pool was a sea of people. I'll never forget it.

9

Walking on Broadway

On a three week tour of Asia with Fulham in the summer of 1966, we stopped off in Singapore to play a friendly game at the Jalan Besar stadium. We'd already taken in Hong Kong, where we'd sailed across the harbour in a junk boat and dined at the famous Floating Restaurant in Aberdeen Bay, and Malaysia, where we'd stayed as guests of the Sultan in Kuala Lumpur.

Nothing we'd seen though, prepared us for the opulence of the Raffles Hotel. The décor was like walking back into the nineteenth century, complete with snake charmers sat behind huge wicker baskets, and pictures from the old Empire days hanging from the walls. We walked into the bar to find the Fulham players sitting in big wicker chairs drinking Singapore Slings. Vic Buckingham, now their manager, was also there with his leg cocked over the arm of his chair, his trademark trilby hat pull down over his head. Spotting myself and team manager Alan Brown, he signalled to us by raising his hat. 'What on earth is he doing,' Alan exclaimed. 'What kind of example does that sort of manager make?'

Within a week of returning to England, we were off again to Bulgaria to play some friendly games in Varna, a picturesque Black Sea resort with long sandy beaches. Our hotel was on the shore, and it was truly idyllic. The street was bustling with fruit and vegetable sellers. One day we went for a walk, going to a stall beforehand to buy a huge bag of peaches. We stopped off at the beach bar and were sat drinking when we noticed a line of huge canvas windbreakers down the shore that were blocking off the view of the other side so we decided to investigate. Grabbing the bag of peaches, we wandered beyond the limits of the fence and peered down from the ledge into a nudist colony. Almost at once, they all looked up at us. We looked back, peach juice dripping down from our mouths.

In order to keep our fitness up, Alan joined us on runs around the town. Though he was ageing, he insisted on leading the group. Being Alan of course, there were rules, such as we weren't allowed to overtake him. As young athletes we could have run past him at any moment, but we daren't, such was his hold over us. As we progressed, the gap between us started to grow tighter and tighter, restricting us to a jog, but we could only go past him once he gave the signal. As the hotel appeared into view, he held his hand up in the air, and we dashed past him to collect our post-run orange juice.

We played two matches, against Spartak Varna and Cherno More. The Varna match was uneventful, but during the match against Cherno, the ball was knocked out from the defence by one of their players and landed in between a defender and Johnny Quinn. Johnny jumped up to meet the bounce but met it a second too late. The defender came in and head-butted him with such ferocity that he passed out in the air and fell down vertically. I ran over to him and looked down. His eyes had rolled back in their sockets. 'Jesus Christ' I swore, and signalled to Alan that we needed assistance.

John came round reasonably quickly but was replaced. As the match restarted, I looked at Alan. He was stood on the touchline, shouting and gesturing, which is something he never did. As I met his gaze he shouted, 'Don. get that bastard. I want him off.'

Alan never swore, and even though I'd long been seen as the hatchet man of the team, it seemed odd for the order to come from him. But if someone needed seeing too, it was probably me who was going to be around to do it. The best time would be when they were concentrating on something else, usually at a corner. But every time the defender got hold of the ball, I heard

Alan from the touchline, 'Get him off this pitch.' He had this defender playing like a frightened rabbit, so I ran over to the touchline. 'Boss, just leave it to me. Don't shout.' But it made no difference. Alan wanted the defender off the pitch no matter what.

Days later, England won the World Cup Final. After celebrating long into the night with the Scandinavian tourists that populated the local bars, we travelled back to the hotel in a horse drawn cart, singing at the top of our voices, 'We've won the World Cup. ENGLAND, ENGLAND.'

*****

All the travelling we did that summer meant that I was unable to take my preliminary coaching badge at Lillishall as I'd originally planned. I'd always wanted to go into coaching and had already done my first course under Lawrie McMenemy at Mosborough. Alan Brown had been very encouraging, letting me lead sessions with school children as part of the club's community outreach. So whilst most pro footballers went back into pre-season training, I travelled to Durham to take my badge with amateur players and school teachers. It worked out really well. Away from the distractions of talking shop with people I knew well, I worked really hard, and passed the course with flying colours.

As a result of Alan's reputation as a coach, Wednesday used to be invited to put on demonstrations of shadow play for other coaches. One of the most memorable occasions was in the summer of 1967 when we travelled to Buxton. Brian Clough had just been appointed manager of Derby Country, and after the training exhibitions had concluded we headed inside, where Brian was due to give a talk on coaching methods. He was slightly more sheepish in those days as he had yet to cultivate the attitude and swagger that would come with his First Division titles.

Alan had coached Brian at Sunderland, and been hugely supportive of him during the time his career ended due to injury, but Brian didn't know that he was going to be there. We were ushered into the room, and sat in the front row. Brian walked in, went up to the podium, and immediately noticed Alan sat right in front of him. Alan held his fist to his face and coughed. Brian gulped. To see his face that day was hilarious.

More commonly we would find ourselves heading down to Lillishall. And soon after I'd graduated from the Preliminary Course, we were invited by Alan Wade, the FA Coaching Director, to put on a display for the Coaching Association Annual Conference. After about ten minutes, Alan called me over and told me to take the reins. We were that good at shadow play by then that we could do it with our eyes closed. It was a good feeling to be in charge.

Wade's assistant at the time was a man called Charles Hughes, who became very influential in football tactics during the 1980s for his adaptations of the Position of Maximum Opportunity (POMO) tactical method. He was a stickler for repetition, and would constantly ask players to do things over and over. When we headed to the pavilion for dinner, Charles stayed behind trying to teach the players in his group something that was far beyond their abilities. We watched him, thinking it was a waste of time, because if you're trying to put something into a session that the players can't do, forget it.

That said, the best thing about putting on a training session is when the players have the skill to pull off what you're trying to teach them. Years later I was at Lillishall with Howard Wilkinson, who was asked to put on a demonstration of how a player could put in a shot on goal on the spur of the moment. Howard set up the players for the demonstration and picked Ian St. John, an ex-international, to be the striker. It was far from a fair test. If you knocked the ball up to Ian, he'd be able to score nine times out of ten. I said to Howard afterwards, 'That was a bit shrewd, Howard. How would you teach players who didn't have the skills to pull that off?'

The next day, we went out for a run. As normal, Alan led from the front, but this time he sprinted so far ahead of us that he disappeared out of sight. Some of the players decided that this was the perfect opportunity to skip the rest of the run and they hitched a lift in the back of a greengrocers van, ducking their heads as they passed Alan. They thought they'd got away with it but at dinner, Alan walked up to Sam Ellis, another of his prodigies. 'You beat me back,' he said. Sam remonstrated, but Alan didn't believe his story, and decided that the only way to settle matter was to have a race. Sam knew that if he lost to Alan, it would prove in Alan's mind that hat he had cheated. Sam was in a state – he couldn't eat anything through nerves. The race never went ahead as Alan stated he was busy, but we all knew that he just wanted to make Sam sweat.

*****

As Cup Finalists we were expected to go places in the 1966-67 season, but our league form was more inconsistent than the previous year. We won only five of our first twenty games, only two of them at home, with goals hard to come by. By the time it got to my 300th game, against Sunderland on March 26th, we'd stabilised in mid table but had little to play for. We were without Peter Eustace and Gerry Young, but still managed to get a 5-0 home win. I scored the goal that put us ahead, a thirty-five yarder from a McCalliog corner. It was the best goal I ever scored that counted.

One of the oddest decisions that Alan made that season, and in his time at Wednesday, was to sell John Hickton to Third Division Middlesbrough. I'll never be able to understand why John didn't become a superstar with Wednesday. Every day I'd see him and Alan working together at Thorncliffe. Often, to prove that John was listening and taking note of what he had to say, Alan would kick a ball downfield and shout, 'John, get the ball.' Without a flicker of an eyelid, John would go and get the ball and bring it back probably not knowing what it was all about.

This went on for a long time until one day Alan kicked the ball. 'Go and get that John.' And he did. He did it about four times. But the fifth time, he didn't. There were no words, just a look. From that moment on, without thinking about it, I can't remember John in the team, he just disappeared. The next time I did think about it was when I heard that he'd left. Middlesbrough had started the season really poorly under Stan

Anderson and were running short of centre halves. It took Stan about five minutes to take the gamble to stick John up front next to John O'Rourke, and he thrived. He scored more than 150 goals for Middlesbrough over the next ten years. It was the biggest clanger that Alan Brown and Wednesday ever made. I rated John that highly.

In his place came John Ritchie from Stoke, who signed for a big fee but never really settled. Alan and Eric agreed to John's demand that he be allowed to live in Stoke and commute to Sheffield daily for training, which was a big mistake. Though he started off well, getting a place in the Football League team, the commute soon became a burden and he lost interest.

Before the season was over, we found out that Ron Springett was going to return to Queens Park Rangers in exchange for his younger brother Peter, regarded as one of the most promising keepers in the game. He'd starred in the League Cup Final against West Brom. With the score at 2-0 he'd made two vital saves, enabling Rodney Marsh to score two goals in ten minutes to draw them level before Mark Lazarus scored the winning goal, and had also helped the club to the Third Division title.

Right until the end, Ron retained the skills that had made him England's number one. Despite not being the tallest of goalkeepers, he had a great command of the six-yard box. At the time, Leeds United's Jack Charlton had a tactic of standing in front of opposing goalkeepers at corners, which made it hard for the goalkeeper to reach the ball. Peter Lorimer would knock in the ball at just the right height for Jack to head the ball. Although it didn't break any rules, most people thought it ran against the spirit of the game. Alan wanted to work out how to combat this. He decided that I would be the one who would take care of Jack. I would stand with him, and when he came out of the box, I would ghost him. Colin Dobson was likewise detailed to track Paul Madeley, another attacking threat.

The next time we played Leeds and conceded a corner, Jack took up his customary position in front of Ron, and I went up alongside him and started jostling. As the ball entered the six-yard box there was a shout of 'Mine.' Ron charged forward, successfully caught the ball, and cleared it up field. Behind him, in the back of the Wednesday net, was Jack looking dazed and confused.

*****

The summer brought a trip to Mexico to play in a round robin competition against Espanyol, Bologna, and Mexican sides Toluca and Club América. When we first arrived, we were treated like kings by the hotel staff and the Mexican FA. In between games, we sunbathed on the top of the hotel, lounging on floating armchairs in the pool and sipping pina colladas. It was stupid really, the sun was so fierce. I remember looking across at Peter Eustace, who had turned beetroot red. 'Peter,' I warned him. 'You've got to get out of this.'

'Ah Meg, you've got to have a little bit of pain to have a decent tan,' he replied.

We also explored the city, though Alan had us on a tight leash. We were told that under no circumstances were we to drink the water, but this didn't stop us from buying ice creams. We were walking down the streets looking very much like tourists, when suddenly, a car pulled up to the side of us. The back window was slowly wound down, and it was Allan. 'What do you think you're doing?' he said. 'I thought I told you not to drink water. What do you think is in the ice cream? Get bloody rid of it.'

All of the games were played in the famous Aztec Stadium and most were day matches, which meant that the heat made everyone irritable. During the Espanyol game, which kicked off at noon, the referee blew his whistle for a decision that Peter Wicks, our goalkeeper, disagreed with. 'Oh **** off referee,' Peter shouted. The referee spun around, dashed towards to Sam Ellis, who he thought was the perpetrator, and sent him off. Sam shouted, 'Meg, he's sending me off.' I remonstrated half heartedly with the referee because Sam was red-haired and really needed to get into the shade before he went crispy. Peter wisely said nothing.

The conditions were really too much for us, and in the space of a week, we lost against Toluca 4-1, the Mexican League 5-0,

Espanyol 2-0, Bologna 1-1, and finished off with a 1-1 draw with Club América. By this time, we were out of the competition and the waiters and warm welcomes had disappeared. Alan and Eric decided that enough was enough, and that we would up sticks and go to New York for a few days.

We stopped off in San Antonio, Texas to catch a connecting flight to JFK. In the middle of the San Antonio terminal was a huge statue of a Texas Ranger, with corridors leading off to the departure lounges. Johnny Quinn and I decided to go for a walk, and couldn't find the way back to our departure lounge. We ended up sprinting down corridors trying to get back to where we started. They held the plane up for us which didn't please Alan.

Once we arrived in New York, we booked into the Americana Hotel, right off Broadway. Having never visited before, we didn't know this, so we went for a walk to try and find it. We saw this cop leaning next to his patrol car and Sam Ellis approached him. 'Good afternoon officer,' he said in his most polite tone. 'Can you tell me where Broadway is please?'

The cop flicks his head up, 'Man you're on it.'

Everywhere we went something exciting was happening. Our first stop was a bar on Broadway. Duke Ellington was sat on the stage playing the piano. Then we went to try and find where Frank Sinatra bought his hats. A little further down the street and we caught sight of a closed nightclub that was holding a party. We peered in. 'Christ.' said Gerry Young. 'That's Jack Dempsey.' And it was. It was his seventieth birthday party, in a night club that he probably owned. Gerry cart-wheeled. The sheer excitement of it all had gone to his head.

*****

After two seasons of going nowhere, it was refreshing that we started the 1967-68 season in good form. We were consistently in the top three until the end of October. The newspapers were full of stories about Wednesday's young team, and how it was starting to fulfil its promise. Right up until Christmas we hung around the top five. But after beating West Ham 3-1 at Hillsborough in early January, we completely collapsed and only just escaped relegation by a couple of points.

The seeds of the collapse were planted in September. Just after a 4-1 home win against Fulham, David Ford was involved in a car crash on Redmires Road. Back then, they used to cover pot holes with pieces of rubber with nails driven through to secure them to the road. David drove over one of them and the car flipped. He broke his knee and his girlfriend tragically died.

Alan Brown really looked after David after that. He'd drive him to training, and then home again. One day, sensing that he was ready to get involved with the first team again, he came up to me and said, 'He's ready now Don. Give him a tester.' In the next training match, I dived into David with a tackle and he hurt his knee again. I felt terrible.

On November 4th we beat Southampton 2-0 at Hillsborough, which put us in an optimistic mood for our next match which was against Chelsea. We travelled down to London knowing that if we won, we'd have a chance of regaining the top spot which we'd held throughout August and again in October. Chelsea had recently upgraded the West Stand at Stamford Bridge and everything was brand new.

We'd not played well, and at half time Alan did his team talk. The frustration in Alan's voice was palpable. There was a tannoy in the corner of the room that was picking up the sound from the stands. Half way through his speech, Alan flicked his eyes up, marched over, ripped the speaker from the wall and threw it in the bath. We lost 3-0.

It came as a complete shock when Alan left the club in February 1968. He'd consistently denied that he was interested in returning to Sunderland but after their manager Ian McColl was sacked, the temptation obviously became too great. When he was asked about the decision in the newspapers, he said that it was one that he'd been mulling over for a while. I imagine now that he'd probably been tapped by the Sunderland Chairman.

Alan's replacement was Jack Marshall, who'd worked under Eric Taylor at Wednesday until Harry Catterick had taken charge. Jack had also been the manager of Blackburn when we'd defeated them in the quarter-final of the FA Cup in 1966. His nickname was 'Jolly Jack.' He had a smile and a nice kind word for everybody. Not just the players, but everybody, from the chairman down to the tea ladies. His party piece was to always have a pocket full of sweets. You'd walk past him and shout, 'Boss.' He'd rummage around in his pocket and then throw you a sweet.

Jack had a reasonable reputation as a manager, but I had been 100 per cent devoted to Alan Brown, who'd been an all-encompassing figure. I honestly didn't rate our team, and without the organisation drilled into us by Alan, I didn't think we'd be able keep up our performance levels. Jack didn't have the strength of character to maintain the discipline and harmony that was needed. In his first team talk, Vic Mobley put his hand up and told him that he wanted to pass the ball around and show people how good he was on the ball. Under Alan's system, he had to get the ball to David Ford as quickly as possible. 'I want to put my foot on it Boss, and play with it.'

'If you want to do that Vic,' Jack replied, 'then you have got license to go and do that. I want you to express yourself.'

I cut in. 'Hold on, hold on. We're not a short ball, lay it up to the midfield and let them turn type of team. We haven't played like that for two or three years.'

Then Jack turned to John Fantham. 'John, I want you to play outside right. Come off the wing and use your speed.' He wanted to bring somebody else in and keep John on the pitch. John nodded his head, 'Yeah. Sure boss.' As soon as the meeting ended though, I heard him whispering, 'I'm not playing on the ****ing wing.'

Being the captain, it was my duty to put him straight. 'What did you say? Look John, if you get in there and say you don't want to play on the wing, then Jack can bring in someone who wants to,' but John mumbled, 'It's ****ing nothing to do with you.'

It was then that I threw a punch. John dodged it, and I got my finger stuck in his tracksuit. We were stuck like that for a few moments, and in that position neither of us were able to get off another punch. We jostled until we both calmed down. Alan hadn't been out of the door for five minutes and already the players were starting to come off the hook.

It was partly Jack's fault. Not long after, we were training in Hillsborough Park. Ian MacFarlane, who was coach, told us that we were going to put full backs on the goal line to try and stop opposition players shooting into the top corner from a free kick. If you put defenders on the line of course, you play all of the opposition strikers onside. 'That's not going to work,' I told him.

'Well that's what we're doing!' Ian said in his thick Scottish accent.

'Well that's fine then Ian. But I don't want to be in that sort of position come Saturday.' We both went to Jack to argue the case, and it turned out that it was his idea. He was, of course, more than happy to accommodate me. 'If you don't want to try it like that Don, you do it how you feel.'

We only won three more matches that season after Alan left. We got to the fifth round of the FA Cup against Chelsea after defeating Plymouth and Swindon, the latter had been Jack's first match in charge. It was a glorious sunny day, and we hadn't won a league game all year. Somehow, Chelsea managed to miss all their chances even though they were ripping us apart. Jack Whitham scored early on, and I managed to put us 2-1 up after I came out of a Chopper Harris tussle and hit a low shot into the corner. They equalised however, and though it looked like we'd improved, we were kicked out in the replay. It was downhill from then on. Our only other wins came in two away matches against Stoke and Wolves.

With my parents, 1944

Ready for a scout trip with First
Brooklands Scout Troop

The school football team. I'm on the back row, second from the left

Standing
to attention
alongside my
PTI colleagues

With Yvonne on
our honeymoon

November 13th, 1959.
With Yvonne and
Gary the evening
before my debut
against Burnley

An early appearance against Manchester City, January 2nd, 1960
© Corbis Images

Rebels with a cause – posing with team mates Gerry Young, Derek
Wilkinson, Johnny Quinn, Jack Martin, and coach Tommy Eggleston on
the Soviet Tour in 1960

A last ditch header saves a certain goal for Sunderland

Sharing a joke with Harry Catterick. Also Pictured are Tom McAnearney,
Alan Finney and Ron Springett

Making the ball safe against Leeds

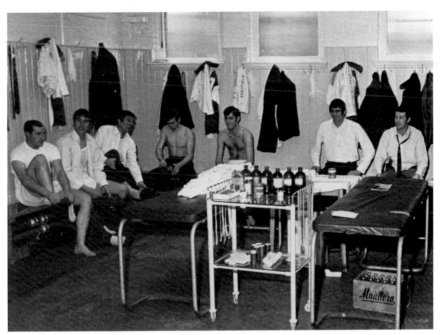

Relaxing in the Wednesday dressing room

Preparing for the new season   Conferring with Alan Brown

A darting interception robs Jimmy Conway of the ball

In front of the brilliant new North Stand with my sons Gary and Neil

Leaving Hillsborough the Sunday that Alan Brown warned me that I'd stand alone in the battle over FA Cup Final tickets

Taking to the Wembley pitch to face Harry Catterick and
Everton on May 14th, 1966

Flipping the coin

The lap of honour. It was crucial for me that we hold our heads high after
the game. Alongside me are Wilf Smith and Johnny Quinn

A rapturous crowd awaited us on our return to Sheffield

Not the best tackle I've ever made. Geoff Hurst is on the receiving end

Taking taking time out as a family

Playing against Manchester United in the late 1960s. Pictured are
Denis Law and Bobby Charlton

Putting the
Wednesday
trainees
through
their paces at
Thorncliffe
training centre

On tour with the
Football League
in New Zealand,
Summer 1969. I'm
in the front row,
first from the right

I had a fine
squad of
players at
Bristol Rovers

Inspecting Eastville with Bill Dogdin and my old teammate Colin Dobson

Sharing a joke during a Rovers training session

Celebrating the Watney Cup win against Sheffield United, July 1972

Eastville wasn't glamourous, but I was proud to serve as Rovers' manager

1979 Portland Timbers

When the opportunity came to manage Portland Timbers, I couldn't resist

Talking to the local press in the Timbers' dressing room

Promoting 'Soccer Fever: Catch It' on the streets of Portland

Results in the early part of the 1980 season did not measure
up to my expectations

With Yvonne on our
fortieth wedding
anniversary

Visiting Hillsborough with
my grandson Simon

Yvonne and myself with Gary, his wife Barbara and their son, Simon

10

Singing Cushie Butterfield

As soon as the season finished, we headed to Austria to play two friendly games against GAZ and Salzburg. It helped us take our mind off things as the scenery was beautiful and Salzburg as nice a city as I'd ever seen. The night of the second game we went to a traditional beer hall. There were big wooden tables and drinking steins lined up on the bar. I spotted a man in the corner waving a union jack and wearing a crombie coat and a deer stalker hat. It was David Niven who was out there filming a movie, I think it was *Before Winter Comes*. Lawrie McMenemy, who was one of our coaches at that time, decided to invite him over for a drink. 'Sorry old boy, filming early in the morning,' David replied.

Then the drinking games started. There was a tradition at the place. A top hat was passed around and when it was placed on someone's head, it was their turn to sing. With a lot of protest, it ended up on Lawrie's head. 'Sing! Sing!' everyone yelled. 'No, No,' Lawrie shouted back in his thick Geordie accent.

There are two famous songs from Newcastle, When the Boat Comes in and Cushie Butterfield by Georgie Ridley. Lawrie relented, and sang them both.

> *'She's a big lass an' a bonny one;*
> *An' she likes her beer;*
> *An, they call her Cushie Butterfield;*
> *An' aw wish she was here!'*

Everyone was in hysterics. Then the traditional chanting and swinging of steins began. Drink! Drink! Drink!

The following month, we travelled to Ireland to play Ards and Glentoran. When we arrived at the hotel, Jack told us that the dress code for the evening meal would be casual dress, but as we walked down the stairs to eat, Eric Taylor sent each of us back up the stairs to get changed. 'Go and put a collar and tie on. It's formal.'

All of us did so, apart from Jim McCalliog. 'You're not my boss,' he told Eric. 'If Jack says I can wear casual, then that's what I'm going to do.' He entered the dining room, and we all looked up at him. Jack walked over and told him that he'd have to go and get changed. 'Is that you telling me, or him?' Jim asked. He ended up eating his meal in the kitchen with the chef. It was the beginning of the end for him at Wednesday.

*****

The 1968-69 season did not start well. Jack fell ill, and had to have a major operation on his appendix. Ian MacFarlane took temporary charge of the team in his absence, with assistance from Lawrie McMenemy. We called them 'The Big Men.'

Ian had been another Alan Brown find, and was proud to have been given the opportunity. His first game was against Manchester United at Hillsborough, with the line up and tactics for the match decided at Jack's bedside. It was a lovely sunny afternoon, and the stadium never looked so good. Somehow, as underdogs, we triumphed 5-4 with a hat trick from Jack Whitham, the most inexperienced player on the pitch. I scored the best goal of my career that day, but it didn't count. It was an absolute screamer but they gave John Fantham offside, even though he was way out on the wing.

After the match Eric Taylor came to see us, and gave Ian a huge hug. I'd never seen him so happy. The newspaper drew a cartoon of the event called 'The Happening,' a copy of which hung at Hillsborough for many years. It was definitely one of the greatest matches ever played at Hillsborough. We crashed back down to earth the next week though in the League Cup, beaten 3-1 by Fourth Division side Exeter. It hammered home just how fragile the team was. I didn't play in the match, but it was one of those weird results. We went on a reasonable run under Ian and stayed around the top half of the table until Christmas.

The atmosphere in the dressing room at that time was really positive, and I was starting to appreciate my position as a senior player. The dressing room was split into two groups, the ones who relieved tension with high spirits, and those who were serious. Jack Whitham was always keeping us up to date with the latest vinyl releases, while David Ford and Johnny Fantham were a constant source of jokes.

Peter Eustace really started to fulfil his promise that season, but his desire for success was giving him itchy feet. He didn't want to be fighting mediocrity every season, and had already asked for a transfer more than once. I always wanted the best for him, but I felt that he regretted his big move to West Ham when it came. He enjoyed being recognised in the Sheffield nightclubs and being part of the scene. In London, he was just another face, and it never really worked out for him down there on the pitch.

Jack Marshall returned to the helm in November but we continued to struggle, in spite of the fact that the club had brought Tom McAnearney back to help him with the day to day running of the club. Tom had spent a couple of years at Aldershot as player-manager and had really turned them around. He had little luck with us though as we lacked fire power. Jack Whitham and Alan Warboys were inexperienced, and John Ritchie was out with a cartilage problem that wouldn't heal. John was handing in transfer requests, as were Vic Mobley and Archie Irvine, who'd been one of Jack's signings.

The fans were starting to get restless. In November, after a defeat to Liverpool at Hillsborough, a number of Wednesday fans were arrested for throwing their seat cushions onto the pitch after the referee disallowed an equaliser. All the Liverpool fans thought it was a goal, as did the linesman, who gave an indifferent shrug when the referee started talking to him. He turned around, gave a strange signal, and then ran up the tunnel.

For a minute chaos ruled, with everyone looking at each other. Then the linesmen followed the referee up the tunnel. The players were left standing about, wondering whether the game had been abandoned. The officials did eventually resume the game but there were constant boos from the crowd. At full time, they were escorted back to the train station in a police car.

It didn't help that just after Christmas, Peter Eustace suffered a freak accident during a secret skiing expedition on the slopes of Stocksbridge golf course, which left us weakened going into February. Jack suspended him, and then put up a note on the door of the training room warning that any player caught skiing, roller skating, horse riding, ice skating or tobogganing would be disciplined. Luckily, the next home game against Leeds was called off due to snow, but Peter was confined to the gym for two weeks.

The axe fell on Jack in March when he was told that his contract would not be renewed. Not wanting to serve his three months notice, he chose to leave with immediate effect. We were at Lilleshall with Tom McAnearney at the time, and he was put in temporary charge after Danny Williams refused to take the job. I remember his first team talk. He gathered us in one of the rooms and stood at the front, leaning on the fireplace smoking a pipe and trying to reassure us. Perhaps because they'd also wanted the job, Ian MacFarlane resigned, and Lawrie was released to take charge of Doncaster Rovers.

It took more than four months to persuade Danny Williams to take the job. He'd had big success at Swindon Town. He'd got them promoted to the Second Division and had beaten Arsenal in the League Cup Final. When I say he was funny, I mean it because he was a real comedian. I'd seen him play on many occasions for Rotherham so I knew him a little, and knew about his successes at Swindon, so it seemed a fair bet. Of course, as a player you never found out the exact intentions behind decisions, so I was never sure whether Danny had been brought in because he was a prospect, or because the club wanted to save money. Certainly, the club had form for finding managers who could thrive on a shoestring.

Things were further confused when, without a manager, we signed Tommy Craig from Aberdeen for £100,000, a record fee for a teenager at the time. The deal had been cooking for six months, and you could understand why. Tommy had a magic wand of a left foot, and was a beautiful passer. He was a flair kind of player, and greatly coveted. In fact he was the kind of player who wouldn't have got anywhere near an Alan Brown team. The night Tommy signed, Eric Taylor went on the TV to say that we had signed an up and coming magician who this club would be built around.

*****

On the day Danny was to be introduced to us, we were told to congregate in front of the North Stand. He turned up, took his coat off, and let it drop to the ground. 'Okay lads,' he said. 'Get up on 'de toes for a bit of star jumping.' I immediately thought, 'He's not a Sheffield Wednesday manager.'

At the end of the previous season, the club had put seven first team players up for sale, and had made big statements about changing the scenery at the club. The problem was that Danny only really seemed to have lower division players on his radar. He wasn't the kind of manager to go up to the board and state, 'I need a centre forward, and he's going to cost £80,000 to £90,000.' A lot of the new players weren't up to the standard of those they were replacing.

I was thirty-four by that time, but still healthy. In ten years I'd never really had a big injury apart from the pulled muscle in my leg. But during a pre-season training session in the summer of 1969, I suddenly felt as though I had been stabbed in the back of the leg. I looked around but there was no one within ten yards of me so I hadn't been kicked. The Doctor taped me up and told me to carry on training but I knew it was bad as my leg kept cramping and I could hardly run.

My injury prevented me from interacting with the other first team players. Some days I would be able to do a twenty minute stint in five-a-sides but usually my leg cramped. Things got so bad that the club let me take Gary, Neil and Yvonne to Blackpool, just so I could get away from the routine of coming into Hillsborough injured. The pull in my calf had spread into my ankle, and I'd developed tendonitis. I spent six months with a heel raise in the back of my shoe, but I wasn't a quarter of the player I had been.

Not long after I sustained the injury, Andrew Stephen, the Chairman, told me that the club had received a request for me to go on an FA Tour of Asia and Oceania under Jimmy Armfield and asked me whether I wanted to go. 'No not really. I'm injured,' I replied. 'Where are Wednesday going?'

Andrew told me that the club were going to Italy, and that it was unlikely that I'd be travelling with them. That was a big hint as to my future with Wednesday so I decided to go to Asia. Alan Hodgkinson, the Sheffield United goalkeeper, was also in the squad, so we arranged to meet on the motorway near Catcliffe and drive down to London together. All the way down, I was thinking that there was no way I was fit enough to play. We trained in Hyde Park, and after about ten minutes of training, Jimmy shouted me over and told me that he was making me the captain of the side.

We flew from England to Los Angeles and on to Tahiti. I had images of palm trees and long sandy beaches in my head, and when we got there we stayed in a resort designed as grass huts around a central building. But the surrounding area consisted of docks and more docks. I sent a postcard to Yvonne saying, 'Believe it or not, this is an island Liverpool.' We played the Tahiti national team in Papeete during a heavy rainstorm. We won the match but got soaked.

Then we flew on to New Zealand, where we played Auckland, Canterbury, Otago and a New Zealand XI in Wellington. The most interesting thing about the trip was learning about the native traditions. We travelled to Rotorua, famed for its sulphur activity, where we hung our cooking pots over geysers and admired the Maori totem poles.

All the opposition teams did a haka before the match, and

sang a farewell song to us before we left. After one game, Ike Robinson, one of the FA officials who travelled with us, decided we were going to do our own going away song, so he clambered towards the front of the coach and started singing 'Now is the Hour.' It immediately became the theme tune of the tour.

'Now is the hour
'For you to say goodbye!'

At the end of every match, our opponents tried to swap shirts with us. We always obliged, meaning that we soon had a load of shirts that we didn't want. It wasn't easy to say, 'Here's your shirt but I don't want yours.' After a 7-1 win against the New Zealand XI we did the same and trod off into the changing room wearing red and white stripes. Five minutes later, a knock came at the door. It was their captain. 'Sorry, we've got to exchange our shirts back again.' It turned out that the shirts had been given to them by Sheffield United, who had toured the previous year, and weren't theirs to give away.

The sun shone all the way through our visit to Singapore and Thailand. After our first training session, Jimmy told us to go back to the hotel to shower and change. The same thing was arranged for the night of the match and we were asked to report in the lobby in casual wear.

Ike and Jack Bowers, another official, had other ideas. Both of them were in their seventies, and Ike turned up in blazer, flannels and trilby, with a raincoat slung over his shoulder. He was appalled to discover that we'd gone casual. 'What are you doing?' he said. 'You're supposed to be dressed formally. You're representing the FA.' They wanted us to get changed but we would have melted.

Then onto Hong Kong where we stayed at a really high class hotel in Repulse Bay and beat the national team 6-0 at Happy Valley. In the press conference before the match, Jimmy Armfield upset the local media, who were under the false assumption that we were the English national team. He tried to placate them by emphasising that we were a strong team, but the media rounded

119

on us in the newspapers.

Towards the end of the match, we noticed that there were some fires being lit in the stands. Jimmy told us that police squadrons were moving into position and that we'd need to leave as soon as the match had finished. 'As soon as the whistle blows, we need to get off the pitch. No waving, no cheering. Just get down the tunnel.' After the match, there were political demonstrations held outside the stadium.

*****

I only played eight games in the 1969-70 season. Every time I trained, Danny would try and convince me to complete the fourteen laps of training he'd put on and play on the Saturday. 'Don't da want to train, Meg?' he'd ask me. I'd remonstrate, saying that sprinting wasn't good for me, but he wouldn't listen. So off I'd go on my fourteen laps on Thursday, and invariably I wouldn't be able to walk by Friday morning. 'Oh Meg, ya'd better play,' he'd say.

The season began with a 4-1 defeat against Manchester City. After the match Danny took to the television screen to deliver his verdict. When asked how many top class players were at Hillsborough, he replied that there were about six.

Even though Danny expanded on what he meant, that he only had six players who he could build a First Division side around, it really set the tone for the season. Danny had probably never had to do a proper television interview in his life, and his style probably took the interviewer by surprise. Come Monday, every player was wondering whether they were one of the players, or whether they weren't good enough. Wilf Smith definitely wasn't happy and Vic Mobley was trying to put a case to an independent tribunal to get away from the club.

Danny's big search was for a new winger, and he eventually signed Tony Coleman from Manchester City for £20,000. Tony never really clicked for us on the pitch, but he was a character, and a big drinker. When he first arrived at the club, he lived with Jack Whitham. They'd go out on a Saturday night, and Jack used to come in on a Monday morning complaining about his behaviour. One day he came in, threw down his coat. 'I cannot live with that man any longer!'

'Well what's he done now?' Tony was always getting Jack into trouble.

'He's come home drunk. He thought the drawer with all my clothes in was a urinal and he's pissed all over my shirts.' T.C. as we used to call him, just laughed and said, 'What's the problem. You can just buy some more.'

At the end of September there was talk of me getting recalled to the first team and I played against West Ham. My muscle played up so I asked not to be picked for the first team, in part so that I could enjoy my testimonial. 11,000 people turned out in the rain to see two games. An Ex-Sheffield Wednesday IX starring Albert Quixall, Dennis Woodhead and Redfern Froggatt played an ex-International team with John Charles, Eddie Quigley and Ron Greenwood. Then a current Wednesday XI played an International XI, with Ron Springett in goal. Sadly, they also saw me limp off the field after sixty-five minutes.

Soon after, John Fantham was sold to Rotherham. He'd been a marvellous servant for Wednesday, and definitely had the talent to play more international games. Since my first game, I had always been a glutton for doing as much as I could for the team. I looked at John on a day when he wasn't feeling it, and I realised I was watching someone who didn't quite have the drive to dictate a game. He was a brilliant golfer, a brilliant tennis player, in fact he was great at everything, but only when he felt like it. Such behaviour wouldn't be tolerated today as players are expected to give 100 per cent commitment just to stand still.

On January 24th, 1970, we played Scunthorpe United in the fourth round of the FA Cup at Hillsborough. There were almost 40,000 people in the ground that day, many of them Scunthorpe fans wearing red and white. In their line up was Kevin Keegan, destined for stardom. We went ahead quickly through Sam Ellis, but goals from John Barker and Nigel Cassidy meant that Wednesday were beaten at home by a Third Division side. I was substituted in what turned out to be my final appearance.

It was an inglorious way to go. I think if I'd been fit, I would have made a difference that season and perhaps Wednesday would have stayed up. There were lots of young players coming in, and they didn't have an anchor to knit them together, which had really been my job for the previous five years.

Not long after I went to see Eric Taylor to ask what the situation was, and that's when management was first discussed. I told him that I'd been considering going to Southend to be assistant to Arthur Rowley. In turn, Eric told me that he was friends with Bert Tann, who'd been with Bristol Rovers for nearly thirty years. 'Don, if you go to Southend I might not see you after twelve months. But if you go with Bert, I might be able to ring you in fifteen years' time and ask you how you're doing at Rovers.' Eric talked to Bert, and it was agreed that I would be allowed to leave on a free as a gesture for services to Wednesday, allowing any club to offer me a contract without having to pay a fee. I went down to Bristol to discuss terms with Bert at Eastville.

When I mentioned how much I was on at Wednesday, I remember Bert saying, 'Well I can't give you that Don, because you'd be on more than me.' I stated that it was what it would take to get me down to Bristol, simply because Southend had already agreed to match my current wages if I went there. Bert obviously wanted me at Rovers, mainly to gain experience to be the next manager, so he agreed to match Southend's offer.

Eastville, as it turned out, was a dog track with a football pitch in the middle, not unlike Owlerton Stadium in Sheffield. There was a hare track that circled the pitch, and flowerbeds behind each goal. On some days after the racing meets, the pitch and the track would be covered in faeces, and we would do our best to skip around them. As I passed the rusting corrugated iron frontage and tired paintwork, I turned to Yvonne and said, 'Jesus Christ, look at this. I can't come here.'

'Well let's go home then,' she replied bluntly.

However, I decided to accept the offer. Walking into Hillsborough on that last afternoon was eerie. I'd already said all my goodbyes that morning and coming back in, after realising that I'd not picked up my boots, the only person around was

Tommy Walker. He was a Wednesday player in the 1930s, and had been dropped for the 1935 FA Cup Final after playing in all the previous rounds. He was in his seventies by that time and working as kit man. It wasn't a grand farewell. I walked away with nothing but my boots to show for eighteen years.

It reminded me of the day soon after Redfern Froggatt had retired, when I saw him outside Hillsborough as I walked towards the players entrance. He was queueing up with the fans at the turnstiles to buy a ticket for the game. Weeks before, he'd been Redfern Froggatt, Wednesday legend, who'd played hundreds of games and scored countless goals. Now he was just another fan. Football is very much 'the king is dead, long live the king.'

11

Gas Head

Having become used to the comforts of life at Wednesday, Bristol Rovers was a culture shock. I wouldn't say I acted snobbishly, but having been used to Eric Taylor's grand tours and overnight stays in big hotels, it took me a little while to realise that I'd been blessed. On the Friday before my first game I travelled down to Bristol with Yvonne and booked into the hotel that the club had arranged for us. It wasn't that nice a place, so we moved down the road to the Grand Hotel.

Later that day, we met the manager, Bill Dodgin, in the lobby. Bill had been manager of the club since the start of the season, taking over from Fred Ford, who'd left to manage Torquay. Bert Tann was General Manager and Secretary, and had managed Bristol for eighteen years up to 1968. Together, they knew the club inside out. After the pleasantries, he asked us if we were ready to go and look round the stadium, so we walked out into the car park where it quickly dawned on me that there was no car waiting. 'No car, Don,' Bill said. 'We're taking the bus.'

Despite my early apprehension, I came to love Bristol. It was such a laid back city even compared to Sheffield, and Rovers were the quintessential family club. Everything was 'Have a nice day.' We returned a couple of weeks later to find a place to live. We made our base at the Hawthorne Hotel and scoured the city but couldn't find anywhere, and it all got a little claustrophobic. So Yvonne decided to go back to Sheffield with the kids and leave me in Bristol to find a house.

On the fifth day of searching, I drove into Fenbrook Close and saw a piece of cardboard in the window of one of the houses saying 'For Sale.' I took one look at it and thought, that's what I'm looking for. The owner was in the front garden mowing the lawn. 'Excuse me, is that right? The house is for sale isn't it?'

'That's right. The price is £8,000. Want to come in and look around?'

'No. I'll have it. It's sold. I'll go and get my Mrs.' Without getting out of the car, I drove all the way to Sheffield, picked up Yvonne, came straight back, and closed the deal. I bought a house without ever going inside it.

*****

My first impression of Bill was of a manager with pedigree as he had managed Southampton and Fulham earlier in his career, as well as a stint in Italy as the coach of Sampdoria. Even though he was in his mid-sixties, he was a fitness fanatic and used to train with us every day, playing in the five-a-sides. He never skimmed a tackle in those matches, and used to take a few knocks from us. But he'd always get back up, inviting us to hit him in the chest as proof of his strength.

Like every sixty-six-year-old manager among twenty-five-year-old players though, he had shortcomings. He was everything you'd expect of a manager of his era, heads down, arses up, and plenty of clichés. 'The Smoke will go up the chimney just the same,' he used to say. He didn't often tell people where to play, or what he wanted them to do. He expected his teams to find the most effective way of utilising its skills. He used to call it 'playing off the cuff'. 'Don't tell people what you want of them,' he told me, 'let them work it out for themselves.'

The practical application of this was that younger players would often show too much enthusiasm in trying to show off their skills. They thought that they were doing well, but it was only when they twigged onto the fact that you actually need to listen to the coach in order to run into the right places at the right times and make the right kinds of passes, that they worked together on the pitch. In one of my first training sessions, I remember telling Bryn Jones and the rest of the players that dribbling wasn't my strong suit, and that passing the ball to me in the eighteen-yard box was a bad idea. 'Just hit a forward pass and get it out of danger.'

I made my début on the 28th of March, 1970 at Eastville in a victory over league leaders Leyton Orient, and the first thing that Bryn did when he got the ball was pass it to my feet while an opposition centre forward was parked next to me in the eighteen-yard box. 'Right Don, got to stay on your toes here,' I thought.

Even though I was effectively playing on one leg, the pace was slow enough that I could just about manage, and I was at ease with the skill level which emphasised positional play over movement. It was a top of the table clash with a lot riding on it, and there were 22,000 people there, which was higher than some of the gates Wednesday were getting at the time.

Signing at the same time as me was Sandy Allen, who'd played European football for Cardiff City. We were the final pieces in Bill's promotion charge, and at that moment it looked on. Orient had been top, and we were chasing right behind along with Luton. We were playing positive attacking football, and Sandy was in match-winning form. But in the last half a dozen games, we only managed one win against Stockport County, who were already relegated. With two games left we were two points behind Orient on fifty-six points, and two in front of Luton in third. Two victories would probably see us promoted, and it was crushing that we lost both games, 2-1 at home to Gillingham and 5-2 away at Tranmere. Orient won both games and Luton got in ahead of us.

For the 1970-71 season, I signed on as player-coach and played roughly twenty games as Bill continued to strengthen the team. In came Robin Stubbs, a talented striker from Torquay, and Kenny Stephens from Walsall on a free transfer. Kenny had previously played in an FA Cup semi-final for West Brom, but hadn't been able to handle life as a First Division footballer. He'd retired in 1968 and opened a newsagents, but Bill and I lured him back into the game. He was still erratic. He could be absolutely brilliant in five-a-sides, and then not replicate the form in games. It was all to do with confidence, and Kenny often needed help with that.

We started well with goals coming regularly. From the beginning of September to early January we went nearly thirty matches unbeaten, but because we kept drawing, we never looked too close to promotion. We also had a great League Cup run, beating Brighton, Newcastle and Norwich on the way to a fantastic 3-0 win over Birmingham City that got us into the quarter-final for the first time, to face Aston Villa. We drew the home match 1-1 with a goal from Stuart Taylor, but lost the replay 1-0. In both games Ray Graydon played magnificently, and attracted the attention of Villa, who agreed a fee of £25,000 in exchange for Brian Godfrey.

It didn't help that we were shaky at the back. In the third match of the season our captain, Tony Ford, had been accidentally kicked in the back by Dick Sheppard, resulting in a chronic condition in his spleen that required medication. Towards the end of the season my injury began to get the better of me. Stuart Taylor and I had started to make a really good pairing and my absence coincided with a drop in form in the last eight games.

One of my main duties as player-coach was to bring Stuart along. He was six foot four, about fifteen stone and good in the air, but he was a gentle giant and he used to exasperate me. A centre forward would bustle him, and it was like a Great Dane going up against a poodle and he'd get knocked all over the place. I used to encourage him to put himself about a bit more, and to challenge harder when centre forwards were treating him forcefully, but I don't think I ever saw him retaliate against another player.

Once I'd retired, my relationship with Bill developed further. I was now his assistant coach, and was supposed to be looking up to him to pick up the skills that I'd need to manage. Already aware of most of his quirks, some of his methods started to drive me crazy. My coaching hero was Alan Brown, who'd stamped his own style, personality, and tactics on his players, but at Bristol, I found it impossible to put across what I wanted to do because Bill was in charge and he was cut from a different cloth. In private, I'd ask him to add more structure to the training sessions and to organise some free kick routines so that we had a better sense of player positioning. 'Let the players make their own decisions on things like that Don,' he told me. 'Let them work it out for themselves.'

'Well Bill.' I'd respond. 'They're going in the wrong bloody places. People might not go in the best places if they're not organised.'

I started to realise that the destiny Bill had in mind for me did not tally with what I intended my coaching career to be. He was training me to be a manager in the style he'd experienced for his entire career. I decided that taking charge of the reserves would be an opportunity to show what I could do. The first team were going through a lean patch at that time, and the reserves were even worse. When I asked Bill, I expected some kind of confrontation but without any resistance at all he said, 'Okay son. If that's what you want.'

I took the responsibility seriously. I immediately looked to the figures who had inspired me, including elements of shadow play into the training. I was conscious of not making the sessions over repetitive as under Alan Brown they had eventually bored the Wednesday players to tears. I knew that the players were playing at Third Division level for a reason, they weren't the greatest in the world, so I wouldn't be able to rely on their uncoached skills to get us through. My approach focused on trying to impart the little pieces of information that the players needed to maximise their potential. They needed to be taught how to lose a man, and how to spin with the ball and go off at a different angle to the defenders. If they executed a move successfully, it was another trick that they'd added to their arsenal.

It was a steep learning curve. I'd only ever been responsible for myself, but a manager was responsible for everything. When we played away matches I had to direct thirteen young lads along with their bags, their kit, and their boots. We'd often get the train from Bristol into London and catch a connecting train to an away game. My assistant would get a taxi with all the luggage and drive straight to the other station, leaving me to get the bus with the players in time to catch the train.

One of the things that impressed me the most was that Bill had been responsible for setting up a coaching academy in South Wales. In charge was Stan Montgomery, a talented centre half for Cardiff in the 1950s, who was a good judge of talent. It was amazing how many players Stan was able to recommend. Towards the end of my time we had seven of them in the first team, and a player at U-21 level for Wales.

It was hard for Rovers to attract players, because Bristol is a bit of a backwater when it comes to football. At Wednesday, you could drive thirty miles in any direction and you'd find any number of clubs, but if I wanted to scout a player or watch the opposition play, I would have to pick and choose games that were important to us. And it was soul destroying when you'd have to leave after twenty minutes because the player you'd been recommended wasn't up to scratch.

Results began to improve. Within a few months I had the players fitter and more organised than they'd ever been, and we shot up the table. I knew that the thought of another season as manager warmed the cockles of Bill's heart, and that he'd never be fully satisfied with reverting back to coach or scout. He knew why Bert had brought me to the club, and because of the good work I'd done with the reserves, Bert thought it was now time for me to take over. I accepted. In my first board meeting, the Chairman and the other directors asked only one thing. 'We've been in the Third Division for thirteen years. Just get us promotion.'

One of the first things I did was speak to Fred Ford, who got in contact and asked if he could have Robin Stubbs. Torquay were in dire straits, and knowing that Robin was one of the club's heroes, Fred thought he might give the club a little lift. What I knew but Fred didn't, was that Robin had developed a bad knee and was past his prime. He hadn't managed to score a goal all season. I warned Fred that I didn't think he'd get many games out of him, but was happy to let him go. 'Oh don't worry Don, we can bandage him up. As long as he's here he can give us a lift.'

'What money are you offering?'

'Oh, we haven't got any money Don. We've got John Rudge. He's got a bad calf, but we could do a swap?'

'That'll do me.'

We arranged to have a practice match at Exeter's ground. I'd watch John and Fred would watch Robin. Both players managed to get through the match, but were limping by half time. As the players went out for the second half, we both laughed.' Bleeding hell, they're both on one leg. Are you sure you want to do it?' There was a moment's silence. 'Yep. Okay. We'll do it.' I got the best end of the deal. Robin hardly played for Torquay, while John proved invaluable for Rovers over the next couple of years.

Only a few weeks after my appointment was officially announced, Bert Tann passed away. It was a big blow to me. Eric Taylor had been spot on when he'd said that Bert was the best person to guide me. He'd managed to persuade me to sign for Bristol when I'd been in two minds, and had placed considerable faith in my potential. I'd told him that I was unsure whether I could manage the administrative demands of the job. 'Don,' he'd said, 'if you have any trouble with that, we can get someone to do it for you. What's most important is that you look the part.'

With that advice in my mind, I gathered the players together for the first team meeting. I walked in and before I could start, my captain Mike Green asked, 'What do we call you now?' Without any hesitation I said, 'Boss.'

The team didn't need all that much changing. Bill had left me with a good squad, but there was a need to bring in more defensively minded players. For three seasons we'd been scoring freely, but we'd also been fragile at the back. I brought in Frankie Prince and Tommy Stanton, who hadn't played all that much under Bill, to add a bit of steel to the midfield, and stop the opposition from playing the ball around

I decided that my first addition to the squad would be a new winger to replace Harold Jarman. Harold had been at Bristol for many years, had scored a lot of goals, and was a fans favourite. They chanted 'Harold' whenever he got the ball. I'd heard that

Colin Dobson was out of the team at Huddersfield. It turned out he had an injured heel, not only could he not train, he couldn't even put his foot on the ground. I asked Huddersfield if I could take a look at him and naturally they said yes. He was in a bad way. As I drove him to Bristol, all he could talk about was how much pain he was in.

There are always little pieces of ingenuity and flair within you that you don't know you have, and on this occasion, I surprised myself. 'Okay Colin,' I said. 'I tell you what I'm going to do. Have you ever tried acupuncture?' The next week, we visited an acupuncturist. He looked at the heel and assessed that the bone was dying. The needles, he said, would be used to stimulate the bone to heal itself. Colin got on the bench and had some needles spun in him. Ten minutes later he got up and walked across the room. He couldn't feel any pain. I had no idea what I was dealing with to be quite honest, it was eerie.

Colin played more than a hundred games for me. As well as getting into good attacking positions, he was great at tracking back to play more defensively as a deep lying winger, and he made so many goals through his skilful crossing. He'd get hold of the ball on the wing and bring it down dead. Then a pass, or a perfectly judged cross that would go exactly where the strikers needed it.

12

Medals in My Eyes

My first season as Rovers manager was mixed, and started with the Watney Cup, a competition organised by the Watney Brewery after they had persuaded the Football Association to change the rules to allow sponsorship for the first time. Entry was based on the top two scoring teams in each division who had not been promoted or entered into European competition at the end of the previous season, a method designed to encourage goalscoring. It was the first competition to introduce penalty shoot-outs at the end of a drawn match.

We beat First Division Wolves at Eastville 2-0, and then Second Division Burnley away in the semi, to set up a final against First Division Sheffield United. There were 20,000 in Eastville on a brilliant sunny day. Before the match began, a parachutist came flying down into the stadium, swooping up and down, positioning himself to land on the centre circle. As he came into land he took the match ball out of a pouch, and as he landed, he placed it on the centre spot. I don't know who organised it, but I remember Bristol City had tried it before, only their parachutist had missed the ground.

For all the talk of it being a competition for goalscorers, the match ended 0-0 and went to penalties. We hadn't been practising penalties with any regularity, because they simply weren't a part of the game back then. All of the first ten penalties were scored, and it went to sudden death. On their seventh penalty, Ted Hemsley walked up and hit the shot to Dick Sheppard's left. Dick dived, smothered the ball, and everything went manic. Dick booted the ball a mile in the air as the fans rushed onto the pitch. We received the trophy, a massive thing, from Roger Bannister who was a big hero of mine.

The Watney Cup was an opportunity to play some good pre-season games with a degree of competition, and get the players ready for the coming season. Of course, it was the first national trophy that the club had ever won, and an achievement that still means a lot to the club. Years later, visiting Bristol for the 125th anniversary of club, I was surprised to hear that the trophy was thought to have been missing, only to have been found in the trophy cabinet of the 1970 winners, Derby County. I was told that Rovers were in the process of securing the trophy permanently.

I was still getting settled when we were drawn against Manchester United in the League Cup. It was another chance to square up against my team, and I was determined that we'd give them a good run for their money. Eastville was packed, and we went ahead through a John Rudge goal, and led right up until three minutes from time before Willie Morgan equalised.

For the replay I recalled Bobby Jones, a Rovers veteran, to add some experience to the side. Again we went ahead when John rushed over to meet a Lindsay Parsons corner and tucked the ball over Alex Stepney's head. Midway through the second half we gave away a penalty when Frankie Prince went through Ian Storey-Moore. 'This is it,' I thought. 'They'll push on now.' I closed my eyes but then I heard the roar from the crowd as Dick Sheppard kept it out.

With three minutes to go, Willie Morgan whipped in a corner that found its way to Sammy McIlroy who headed in. It looked as if it was going to extra time, but with moments left we got a corner. Kenny Stephens knocked it in, and Bruce Bannister reacted faster than anyone else to slot home. The fans went mad in the away stand. It was the highlight of the season and definitely one of my proudest moments. I'd gone up against the best, and I'd proved I had what it took to manage a team in that environment.

The next month, I lost Wayne Jones during a match at Brentford. Wayne was a real flair player and had just been called up to the Wales squad for the first time. He was running along as normal when, all of a sudden, he stumbled to the ground clutching his knee. The doctors initially thought it was a cartilage injury, but it turned out to be crepitus, and they told him that if he didn't stop playing immediately, he'd end up with a fused leg. Because Wayne was under contract as a player and didn't have anything to do, he started shadowing my assistant Bobby Campbell. Bobby had been a great player for Chelsea and Reading after the war, and had won Scotland caps. After retiring, he had chosen to become a physiotherapist. He taught Wayne all he knew, sent him on courses, and eventually Wayne also became a full time physiotherapist.

Bobby was a good coach and a great laugh. Whenever we had a good result we used to have a few drinks, and when Bobby drank he used to start waxing lyrical about how Scotland was the greatest country in the world. Eventually I'd remind him, 'Bobby, you've been down here forty years, it can't be that good. If you love it that much, why don't you go back?' He wouldn't pay any attention of course. Instead, he'd rush to the front of the coach, grab hold of a microphone, and start singing 'The Northern Lights of Old Aberdeen.'

Just after Christmas, Dick Sheppard had a horrific incident during a match against Tranmere Rovers. Dick was a brave goalkeeper, but on this occasion, his bravery had led to him getting kicked on the head when going down to make a save at the feet of a centre forward. He was immediately stretchered off the pitch and shipped to Frenchay Hospital, where it was revealed he had a depressed skull fracture. I went to see him as soon as the game finished and he was already in the operating theatre. They told his wife and I that they'd had to place an umbrella instrument in his skull to pull out the depression.

A couple of days later I was sat in my office at Eastville with local Rovers journalist Robin Perry, who'd come to ask me what the situation was. I told him I was looking for a replacement. 'It's going to be touch and go whether Dick ever plays again.'

I had Malcolm Dalrymple, who had taken over temporarily, and also Richard Crabtree who had great shot stopping and distribution skills, but at five foot seven was too short for my liking. Richard's lack of reach meant that he was always getting caught by shots into the top corners of the net. It was then that Robin told me about Jim Eadie, a Scottish goalkeeper at Cardiff. Jim had disciplinary issues, and had exasperated their manager Jimmy Scoular to such an extent that Jimmy had kicked him out of the club. 'He's recently run a red light and he's in trouble. Jimmy wants rid of him.'

'Have you ever seen him play?'

'No, I don't know anything about him, but he's played in the first team.'

I pulled down my copy of the Rothmans League Book from a shelf. Jim had reasonable pedigree and importantly, was six foot three. Over the next few days, I asked around, and everyone told me that he was trouble. Given that I didn't have much of a choice, I decided to gamble. I gave Jimmy Scoular a ring: 'Do you want to get rid of him?'

'Not half. I can't get rid of him quick enough.'

'Right, I'll take him. I'm on my way.'

I drove to Cardiff and signed Jim there and then. It turned out he was the best kicker I ever had. He was so good that he often had to take some of the energy out of his kicks to ensure that they didn't shoot out of the stadium. But he was tricky to manage. 'You'll be playing on Saturday Jim,' I told him on his first day at the club. 'Make sure you wear a collar and tie. On the Saturday, he turned up without a tie because he didn't own one. He smoked like a chimney and to encourage him to stop I started fining him – money for the Christmas party. Many a time, I'd look over my shoulder on the team coach and see smoke rising up into the air from the back seats.

I tried everything I could to help Dick get back into the first team, knowing full well that he shouldn't really be there. In the reserves, he'd get upset because I wouldn't give him a chance. It was really difficult to explain to him that he'd done nothing wrong, and that I couldn't take a risk dropping a form player.

135

You don't come back from those types of injuries and his brain just wasn't in sync. He would come to catch balls and miss them by miles. I loaned him to Torquay where he played a couple of games, but it was another year before he played for Rovers again, in a derby against Bristol City in December 1974. He conceded four goals in the second half and retired soon after.

In March, I made the vital signing of Alan Warboys from Sheffield United. I'd already got Bruce Bannister, who Bill had signed for a record fee, but being a fan of the 'one big one, one small' combination, I decided I needed a big centre forward to lead the line. I found out that Alan was available for £38,000. I thought, 'We can't afford that.' So I went to the board and told them straight. 'I know it's a lot of money, and that it would be a record fee, but Alan would put the icing on the cake.' I was delighted when they told me to go and see what I could do.

I went up to Sheffield and met John Harris, United's manager, and we cut a deal. I also met up with John Fantham, who'd played alongside Alan at Wednesday. 'Why the hell have you signed him, he's a donkey?' he said. Of course, Alan was no donkey. John remembered Alan as a young kid, trying to get to grips with the First Division in a struggling team. I wanted to take an older Alan down to the Third Division, where I believed he would prosper.

That night, I rang John Harris. 'John, the deal is done.' The last thing he said to me before he put the phone down was, 'That is clear isn't it Don?' Not having much experience with transfer fees, I was unsure what he meant by 'clear.' I asked Bill. Turned out that clear meant that if a player had any add-ons on their current contract, the buying club agreed to pay them to get the player. I got back on the phone to John: 'You crafty old bugger.'

*****

The Club President of Rovers was the Duke of Beaufort, the Queen's Master of the Horses, and in the summer of 1973 we were invited to tour Beaufort Hall in Badminton. We played a five-a-side competition on the lawn against the jockeys of the

Beaufort Hunt and were given a tour of the house, which was a real antique. The first room we walked into contained a huge parrot cage, and the floor was covered in nut shell. Adjacent to that was the mail hall, where the sport of badminton had been invented. We walked through into another room where we were introduced to the Duchess, who was wearing a large wig that sat at a wonky angle. 'Oh do come in,' she said.

While I spoke to the duchess, Colin Dobson's wife Suzanne spoke to the Duke, who began showing her a large painting of himself sat on a horse with the Queen and Prince Philip in the background, and some photographs of Prince Charles. As Suzanne scanned the pictures, she noticed a photograph of the Duke with Basil Brush. Keeping a straight face, she asked. 'Is this a member of the Royal Family too?' 'Oh no dear,' the Duke replied. 'That's just an entertainer.'

That season, the club reverted back to its classic blue and white quartered blue shirts. It was the first of many initiatives instigated by Rovers' new Public Relations Officer, Keith Hunt, whose priorities for the team were very different from mine. The season began well. Alan and Bruce continued to perform well together, and thanks to their goals, we went on a twenty-seven match unbeaten run. Bruce lived in Doncaster and Alan in Leeds, and they used to meet up on the A1 and drive down to Bristol together. In order to promote the club, Keith coined the pair 'Smash and Grab' and had Wild West style posters made of the two which were distributed around the city.

The first match to take place after the poster initiative began was an away trip to Brighton, where Brian Clough had just taken over. The match received a lot of attention because all of the matches that day had been called off as a result of icy weather. We beat them 8-2, the perfect away performance. Alan scored four goals, Bruce three, and Gordon Fearnley the other. After the match, I went into the press room to do an interview. Brian was giving his interview on the other side of the room and gave us no credit at all. It was all about how crap his team had played, and that none of his players had the heart of a thimble. I congratulated my players while trying not to give them so much praise that they forgot themselves. We played Brighton at home later in the season, and by that time Brian had improved the side a lot.

I didn't dislike Brian, but for one reason or another we always clashed. On one occasion he rang to tell me that he was interested in taking Stuart Taylor to Nottingham Forest, but his offer was so small that I decided to reject it. The next time we played Forest, Brian was sat on his bench when Stuart let a Forest player dispossess him. Brian looked to his assistant Jimmy Cox and bellowed loudly, 'I'm glad we didn't go and take him, Jimmy.' A few minutes later, Stuart made another mistake. 'Yup Jimmy. We did the right thing not taking him.'

'Hey Brian,' I shouted. 'Just one of your players cost twice as much as all of my team, so shut yer ****ing mouth or I'll come over there and knock you straight off that bench'

Without taking his eyes off the game Brian said, 'I'll expect an apology on Monday morning, Donald.' I realised that I shouldn't have cursed. So I told my secretary to send a letter to Forest saying that I was sorry for the spat, trying to show that I was the bigger man.

By Christmas, I felt that promotion was a real possibility. Gates were up, and we were playing some fantastic football. It was then that Keith Hunt asked me whether I was interested in taking the team on an end of season tour. Knowing how profitable the tours at Wednesday had been, I said yes. Keith told me that because Australia had qualified for the World Cup, and wanted to arrange some warm up matches against good opposition, they had invited the British FA to send a team over. We accepted, and matches in Sydney, Melbourne and Brisbane were arranged, as well as matches in Hong Kong, Singapore and Thailand. 'We'll make a mint,' Keith reassured me.

In order to promote the tour, Keith decided that it would be a good idea for us to make a record and release it in Australia before we arrived. He paid for some recording time in a studio on Carnaby Street in London, and hired Rod Hull and Emu to sing along with the team. When we arrived, I sat in the control booth and watched the team sing, 'We'll be Singing Bristol

Rovers All the Way' to the tune of 'She'll be Coming Round the Mountain.' It was dire. The players had fun, but the song didn't stand a chance of getting into the Top Ten.

I started to get linked with other clubs. In January 1974 we played Nottingham Forest in the third round of the FA Cup. We'd drawn the game and played well. Afterwards, I found myself in the Forest tea room. Wednesday used to have a scout for the Midlands and he happened to be there. We got talking about Derek Dooley, who'd been sacked as manager on the previous Christmas Eve. He asked me, 'So are you coming home son?'

I didn't realise it at the time, but I was being tapped up by Wednesday. I'd not applied for the job, but I'm sure now that they'd sent someone to test the water to see if I wanted to go. The next day, the phone rang and it was Lawrie McMenemy. 'Don, you've got medals in your eyes haven't you. You're not staying at Rovers to get a Championship medal are you?' I was confused, and asked him what he meant. He replied, 'Well, what's happening with Wednesday. That's twice you've done that.'

Lawrie also knew that Norwich had been interested in me, and apparently I'd turned that job down as well, though actually I hadn't, I just thought that people had been pulling my leg when they'd mentioned that they wanted me as manager. I'm confident I was being considered for the Wednesday job, and I've kicked myself ever since for not applying. I'd gone back to Hillsborough earlier that season with Rovers, and looked at the ground from the dugout thinking what I had at Bristol Rovers, and what I could have.

It wasn't long after that my brother Cyril passed away. Like my father, he suffered from diabetes, though his prognosis was more severe. For many people who suffer from the disease, it's a case of following a diet and taking the right doses of insulin, but Cyril really suffered. After he'd finished playing football, he and his wife, who was also called Yvonne, had decided to take the inheritance they'd received from her mother and open a guest house in Newquay. Their place was right next to the bus station and did a roaring trade.

One day, Yvonne called and told me that Cyril was in a real bad way in hospital and the doctors were fearful. I had a Rover car at the time, and I pushed it to its limits that night, driving from Bristol to Newquay in less than two hours. Cyril looked so poorly, with his face swollen up due to a kidney problem. He came back from that, but about two weeks later, Yvonne called again and told me that he had passed on. He was only forty-four.

*****

Our form inevitably came back down to earth after Alan Warboys suffered an injury, and the unbeaten run came to an end. I'd bought in Dave Staniforth from Sheffield United to bolster the attack, but he wasn't as prolific as Alan had been. At the same time, Oldham started on an unbeaten run and pipped us to the Championship. Having wanted to win the League, it was a disappointment.

We finally got the points we needed for promotion away at Southend. It was a Friday night match, and hundreds of Rovers fans made the journey. At full time they stormed the pitch. We made our way up to the Directors Box to wave to the crowd. I was stood there with the team when it suddenly crossed my mind that this was Bill's achievement as much as mine. I went down into Southend's boardroom, grabbed Bill and took him back up with me. With the Bristol fans looking on, I lifted Bill's arm up. He turned to me, and with tears in his eyes, said, 'I'll never forget this son.' But he did!

A couple of weeks later, club secretary Pete Terry told me, 'You'll get some big praise at the next meeting Don.' We'd got promoted, gates were up, and everything was going great. 'You're right,' I said. 'I probably will.' Rovers were a very old fashioned kind of club. Before each board meeting we'd have a meal, which usually consisted of baron of beef with piesporter wine. I would give a little talk on how the club was going, and they would ask me questions on the playing side. On that occasion the meeting proceeded as usual. We finished the meal, and started talking business. Pete had thought that the Chairman would then stand up and say, 'You know, we're very pleased with the job that Don is doing, I think we should have a round of applause.'

But before that could happen, a Director who had been placed on the board to represent the supporters club stood up. 'I have a complaint. We have lost our fund-raising money by you taking the pies off us.' The supporters club used to have a pie stall at the back of the stand which they used to raise money. It turned out that Keith Hunt had taken the stall off them in order to boost income for the club. Keith and the Director had it out over who was going to sell the pies the following season, So much so that the meeting ended without me getting a mention.

*****

Foreign tours were second nature for me, but for the Rovers players the trip to Australia was a big deal. Though the Rod Hull record was best left forgotten, it had created a little bit of hype among the fans and the players were buoyant. As an experience, it couldn't be topped, but as a money-making exercise for the club it was a complete bust and things went wrong from the start. Even before we'd landed, we heard news that the match against the Australian National Team, the centrepiece of the tour and the main reason we were there, had been called off. A few days earlier, the Socceroos had played Honved, one of the biggest teams in Hungary, and one of their players had punched an Australian and broken his jaw. The Australian FA responded by withdrawing the national team from all friendly matches in the lead up to the World Cup for safety reasons. It was their first World Cup and they didn't want to travel with walking wounded. Instead, we played a Queensland XI and lost money.

In terms of matches, we had a reasonable time. Most of them were won by heavy margins, and I was able to try out a few combinations and formations against reasonable opponents. The only exception was the match against Victoria State. The night before, the players decided to go out for a drink. A number of them took things a little too far and turned up the next day hungover. Though we were 1-0 up at half time we were playing terribly, and I was furious.

Before the match, the organisers had asked me if they could install some recording devices into the dressing room, so that Australian football fans could hear what a British half time team team-talk sounded like. I agreed, in the belief that we'd follow the trend of our previous matches, and that I'd be able to say some thought provoking things. Come half time however, I marched the players into the dressing room, and slammed the door behind me. I was ready to take a bite out of them, and completely forgot that I was being recorded. Out came a river of insults. 'You ****ing lot,' I shouted. 'You do realise that you're not just playing for Bristol Rovers. You've also got a Union Jack on your back.'

By that time I was annoyed with the players because they weren't taking the tour as seriously as they should be. I'd been told that some of them had brought women into our section of the hotel after a game, and as a response, I decided to teach the team a lesson. As we gathered in the lobby to leave for the airport, the reception phone rang. The receptionist shouted, 'Mr Megson, Mr Megson, Bristol Rovers, there is a phone call for you.'

I picked up the phone. 'That's awful,' I said. 'So it's very serious is it?' As I spoke the team gathered round me, assuming that I was about to give them bad news. 'That was the police,' I told them. 'Three girls have gone into the police station and complained about untoward behaviour by Bristol Rovers players, so we can't leave. We're here until it gets sorted out which could be ages, even months. The police have said that I need to take your passports

The players handed over their passports. 'No point in the whole team being accused,' I went on. 'I need to know the three lads who were involved.' The players started spluttering. 'Hey, I had a girl in my room but I never laid a finger on her.' 'You can't say that I had a girl in my room. That'll get back home and the wife will divorce me.'

I had three confessions. The phone rang again. 'Don't worry sergeant,' I said. 'I'm trying to get to the bottom of it, so that the three players you're after will be available to be interviewed.' I put the phone down. I looked into players eyes and then to the far side of the lobby. All of a sudden John Rudge walked around the corner with a big grin on his face and walked over to stand next to me. John had been the person on the other end of the line. It was just a joke, but it had a really serious lesson behind it. Not the best moment for me or the team though.

As our time in Australia drew to a close, we really started to run low on money. In an effort to generate some more income, I contacted the brother of ex-Wednesday goalkeeper Roy McLaren, who was the manager of a team in Newcastle, a town on the south coast. I told the Rovers chairman we'd got a game, but I had no real knowledge of where we were going, or what the match would be like. When we arrived, it turned out that the club had no real stadium, and no real changing facilities. I watched the match from a grass verge by the side of the pitch. We won 9-2 but it was a pointless exercise.

On the way back to Britain we stopped off in Hong Kong. The match there was a failure as none of the locals came to watch. 'Don't worry Don,' Keith reassured me. 'We'll make a mint off the game in Bangkok. It'll be a massive 60,000 gate.' Although the gate for that match was impressive, the tickets were priced at the equivalent of 5p, meaning that we once gain lost money. Looking back, I shudder, when I think of how many players I could have bought if we'd just stayed at home.

In following years, Rovers tours were more modest affairs. The next year I was asked if I'd like to take a team to Holland. Thinking that the lads would enjoy it, I accepted. 'There's not a lot of money though Don,' the board reminded me. 'Keep it tight.'

And tight it was. The match was to be played just over the Belgian border into Holland. We travelled over to Holland on the day, played the game, and then drove back over the border to stay in a Belgian hotel for the night, as Belgium was slightly cheaper. The next day, we drove home. That's the way it was for lower league teams at the time. If you were in the First Division, you'd stay in first class hotels and be treated well. If you were in the lower leagues, you'd travel overnight, get a bag of chips, and stay in bed and breakfasts. That was the reality.

13

Treading Water

As far back as I can remember, my son Gary always had a football at his feet. As a young boy, I'd take him and his brother Neil up to a pitch near King Edward VII School. It wasn't anything remarkable, but behind one of the goals was a steep grass bank which meant that the ball would always roll back to you if you hit a wayward shot. Both boys had talent, but it always appeared to me that Gary showed the most enthusiasm. He never wanted to be anything apart from a footballer. He had good movement and wanted the ball as much as possible. It wasn't long before he started playing for his school team at Malin Bridge in Hillsborough, and Yvonne and I would often watch him.

Although Yvonne wasn't a big football fan, she followed it as a consequence of my career. She was the typical proud mother on the touchline, cheering on her sons. I remember when Gary played his first ever game, he forgot to take his boots. I hopped back in the car to go and get them, but by the time I returned he'd borrowed a pair and the game had begun. I'd missed the first ten minutes and apparently, in my absence, Gary had shirked a tackle. Yvonne had shouted, 'Get stuck in' to which Gary had said something out of turn. Yvonne had run onto the pitch with her umbrella. 'First of all, don't talk to me like that,' she'd said. 'Secondly, don't pull out of tackles.' She'd heard me say the same things to him, and wanted him to succeed as much as I did.

Football journalists used to say that going up against me in a challenge was like putting your foot in a bear trap. I never pulled out of tackles, they said, and used to cart people around. I don't think that was the case. I never considered myself a dirty player, and neither did my team mates. They did consider me to be the enforcer of the team, the player that would look after you, and take a few beatings on your behalf, but nothing malicious. Gary on the other hand, never went into strongarm tackles. He took care of himself on the pitch, and didn't stick his head in unless it was completely necessary. It was nothing to do with bravery as all players play the game in their own way.

Neil was a bit of a dreamer and slightly harder to read. He was a reasonable sportsman, but life held too much interest for him to be pinned down to one thing. If something caught his interest, then his concentration would slip from one thing to the other. As a consequence, I never remember him showing much of an interest in being a footballer. More recently however, he's told me that he did.

I was determined that Gary wasn't going to get any favours from me in football just because he was my son. Even so, I wasn't prepared for Bill Dodgin's decision to pass on him when the time came to take on apprentices. I knew that Gary had the talent to make it if he wanted. Doug Hillard had recently taken over as manager of Mangotsfield and he agreed to give Gary a game. Not long after that, I received a phone call from Tony Waiters, the manager of Plymouth. They'd scouted Gary during a Mangotsfield game and Tony was interested in taking him. 'I suppose he's with you is he?' he asked.

'No Tony, he isn't,' I replied. 'If you want him, take him.' So Gary went down to Plymouth. It just so happened that Alan Brown was working there as Assistant Manager so I wonder at the back of my mind whether Alan had something to do with it. It was funny. Gary was around fifteen at the time, as I had been when Alan Brown was coaching at Wednesday.

*****

After the joy of promotion came the reality of life in the Second

Division. From a personal point of view, it was initially a great experience. For one, I'd proved that I had what it took to be a good manager. I'd put together a fluent side, and I wanted to show them off. And although Alan Warboys had been injured for much of the second half of the season, the hype around him and Bruce was still charged. But now we were playing against teams like Fulham, Sheffield Wednesday, and even Manchester United. Not being cynical, but in many ways I'd set myself up for the sack. Suddenly, the fans had more ambition, thinking that we were going to do all sorts of things, maybe even get promoted to the First Division.

It was a story we've all heard before. The fans and I were on a high, but as struggled for points, our relationship started to turn sour. Apart from anything, the team simply wasn't good enough for the Second Division. I knew it wasn't good enough. If you sat down and gave an honest answer, we weren't really talented enough to create the chances for Alan and Bruce to score the goals they had the previous year. Colin Dobson wasn't really committed to the first team in the way he had been previously. He was a year older, and wanted to take on more coaching responsibility. Frankie Prince and Tommy Stanton were not talented enough on the ball to be the creative force we needed in that league. At Second Division level you needed to have skill to create chances from the midfield.

That's not to degrade Frankie and Tommy's talent, which was considerable. But I could only train them to be the best players they could be, not the best players in the league. They were vital to my set up, but there's only so far you can go with steel. Chances are that if they hadn't clicked, I would have been remembered differently. 'Well Megson had Prince and Stanton in midfield and they couldn't pass for toffee.' But because the tactics had worked, I was considered a good manager and they were considered to be good players. 'They work hard,' the fans would say, 'they graft every day, and try for every ball.'

The crucial thing to understand as a football fan is that if a manager can't get players in to revitalise and renew the team, then a club is going to stand still. If a club in that situation sells, then you're asking for trouble. I was faced with going from God's gift to pariah, because Bristol had become a club that hovered in the relegation places every year. The board wanted me to get rid of players to raise money and of course, other teams don't come in for your cast offs, they only want your best players. Within two seasons, I'd sold both Bruce and Alan, and the fans had started to ask where the goals were going to come from.

Part of the blame lay with Keith Hunt. It was hard for me to hear the Chairman say that I had no money for players when I knew that money was being wasted. At one meeting, I found out that the Chairman had selected an artist to paint a picture of the Duke of Beaufort to go on the wall in the board room which cost £750. Another time he decided that the club needed to find a new ground, so he spent £5,000 on a survey looking for possible sites. I understood that the Chairman had his own responsibilities, but I knew that the team had to strengthen, and that the money could be used better on the squad.

One of the things I introduced when we got into the Second Division, in order to make the team feel professional, was a pre-match lunch. Before each home game, I gathered the players together at The Crest, a hotel on the outskirts of the city. There were two benefits. Firstly, I was able to keep an eye on what they were eating pre-match. Secondly, it enabled me to sit down with each player and talk to them about their responsibilities. I thought it was great. The Board however, was sceptical, and couldn't understand why I was spending the club's money feeding the players. The players, it turned out, hated it. After a year, Mike Green asked me, 'Do we have to do this boss?' It transpired that all the players preferred to have their pre-match lunch with their families.

The end of the season came down to a last day survival battle between us and Cardiff. We travelled down to Millwall knowing that if Cardiff won and we lost, we would go down. The atmosphere was tense and before the game I went into the dressing room toilets. The cubicle walls didn't go all the way to the ceiling – there was a little gap at the top – and coming out of that gap was smoke. I stood on the seat in the next cubicle along and looked over the top. There was Jim, puffing away on a cigarette, his fingers stained brown. 'Fiver please Jim,' I said. The game was tight, with chances at both ends, and going into injury time the score was one all. Then, we had a penalty awarded against us. Jim saved it and we came off the field to find out that Cardiff had lost. Jim had gone from villain to hero.

Earlier in the season, I booked onto an FA coaching course at Loughborough to get my full coaching badge. I'd attended the previous two years, and had told Allan Wade that I was all set to attend. But two weeks before I was due to go, Bill Astbury, a coach, asked me if I wanted to go on a tour of Rhodesia with a team sponsored by Lexington Cigarettes. 'There's £1,000 in it for you if you want to go,' he said. After such a difficult season, I decided to take him up on the offer.

It was a hilarious tour. We played four teams in Bulawayo and Harare, then known as Salisbury. We also stayed at the Hwange Game Reserve, halfway between Bulawayo and Victoria Falls, in a hotel built around a waterhole. Every day the elephants would walk onto the grounds and we'd watch them from the balcony. There were fourteen coaches, including Roger Hunt of Liverpool and Ernie Hunt of Coventry. We did a little coaching, played a few matches, and generally had a good time. One of the stipulations of the tour contract was that our team had to include two Rhodesians in its starting line-up. As they weren't too skilled as players, we often substituted them off after ten minutes.

*****

With money so tight at Rovers, I was forced to innovate. One day I was taking training at Frenchay Cricket Ground, and had the players do some shooting practice. There was nothing behind the net except for hawthorn bushes, and if someone hit the ball too hard, it would sail over the top and onto farmland on the other side. We would then have to scramble through the bushes to the other side to get it back. It was a good patch of land, and over the next couple of weeks I thought about the prospect of the club buying some of the land and turning it into a training ground. Eventually, I approached the farmer who liked the idea so we did it. Years later, when Rovers were in dire straits, they sold the land to a supermarket chain and made a lot of money when they needed it.

Realising that it wasn't enough to rely on Stan Montgomery and the South Wales academy, I tried to recreate the arrangement in the Northeast. I got in touch with a club in Consett, near Newcastle, and drove up to do a deal. I agreed that Rovers would give them some money, and in return, they agreed to give us first refusal on any players they uncovered. The problem was that Rovers was operating on a shoestring, and Newcastle and Sunderland always had the eyes of the locals. I spent hours driving back through the night to Bristol for training the next morning, and by the time I got back, I'd decided that the idea was unsustainable, and nothing ever came of it.

As an alternative, I decided to set up a schoolboy team. I didn't have any players to get it off the ground so I started with the sons of ex-Rovers players. There were John Pett's two sons, Doug Hillard's son Gary, and the Mabbutt brothers, Kevin and Gary. Kevin soon made the decision to move to Bristol City, something his father had wanted. I was worried that I'd lose both brothers, so I was relieved when their father decided that he would be happy to have one with one club and one with the other. It turned out that I had the best deal. I initially thought Gary was going to make a centre forward, but of course, he ended up as a defender.

Setting up a good youth policy is an important part of being a good manager, but it rarely benefits the person who sets it up. A good example for me was Ian Holloway. Both City and Rovers were aware that he had potential, and City believed that they could win him over by showing that they were the bigger club, but I took a different approach. I decided to play him in a game in the reserves against the first team at Eastville, to demonstrate that we were serious about his development. Talking to him since then, it turned out that it was the thing that swung his decision towards Rovers.

We still had a number of good players in the club. David

Williams, who made his first team début in 1975, was a very talented midfielder who spent ten years at the club. He had a career as a teacher, and spent four years with us as a semi-pro. It was Colin who really pushed him. I'd long since put him in charge of the reserves, and after a few months of David playing there, Colin started to highlight David as a prospect: 'You know that David Williams? He's far too good for the reserves. Take a look at him.'

Colin was right. He was a Bobby Moore type combative midfielder, and light years ahead of reserve quality. I fast-tracked him into the first team and he soon became a regular. At first he was happy to remain a teacher, but after a year in the first team, his head got turned. Other clubs were starting to take an interest, and I was faced with the possibility of having him poached from under me because I couldn't really offer him much. He had his teacher's salary in addition to the money he was making from his part-time wage. So I approached the board with a plea for them to match his current earnings, which was around £90 a week. They initially rejected it, to which I responded that they didn't want to take the chance on someone else coming in and taking him. They relented, but the only problem now was that David immediately became the highest paid player at the club.

*****

In the spring of 1977, Brian Tiler, the manager of Portland Timbers in the North American Soccer League, came to visit me with his scout Les Rigby, and asked if I had any players I could loan him for the season. I was Wednesday's captain when Brian had been captain of Rotherham, and we used to organise golf matches between the two clubs so I knew him well.

I'd just lost Mike Green to Plymouth and needing a centre half, I'd signed Graham Day from Forest Green. He had rough edges but was quick and keen to learn. In order to aid his development, I decided that it wouldn't be bad to let him go over and experience a season with professionals, provided he was back for the start of our next season. Portland ended up getting to the play-offs, which meant that he stayed in America longer, which was infuriating because I needed him as backup for the end of season run in.

Rather than ask for money, I decided it would be better for a few other players I was bringing through if we visited Portland to play a friendly, and split the gate receipts. So after the season ended we went to Portland. While I was there I met the head of the Timbers board, Keith Williams. He was a rich man and took us all for a trip on his yacht. We got on well. We had a great week, and we made money out of the match gates. I decided to stay an extra week with Brian and have a holiday.

The 1977-78 season did not look promising. We were really down to the bones by that time and in dire need of some fresh strikers. In desperation I took on Bobby Gould. He'd been a top league player but was coming to the end of his career. He lived in Bristol so it seemed like a good match, and after he scored a hat trick in his first game it seemed like good business. I don't think he scored after that though.

Early in the season, I sent the reserves to play against Frome. Playing for Frome was Paul Randall, and he tore our defence to pieces. Colin Dobson and I were watching the game and at half time I said, 'Who the hell is he? He can bloody play can't he.' Afterwards, I spoke to Paul and found out that he was stacking shelves in a supermarket. He'd had trials at Torquay and Bristol City, but nothing had come of them.

I had to have him, so I went to the board. A couple of weeks before they'd told me that the budget wouldn't allow for another signing, and they refused again. I was desperate, and even offered to pay Paul's wages for a while in return for a slice of the transfer fee when he left us. The board initially said no, but the next morning the Chairman rang me. 'I've had a word with the board members and we'll let you sign him.' Paul played about ten games for me before I left the club, and hit in goals left, right and centre before he transferred to Stoke for £180,000 halfway through the following season.

My other shining light was Andrew Evans, and it personally hurt me when he had to retire. He was extraordinarily fast and skilful on the ball. His one failing was that he had a tendency to jump out of tackles. I tried to push him, telling him that he had to be braver and more physical. But during a game against Southampton, he brought a ball down and Mike Pickering, their centre half, came right through him and took his ankle right out. The bone was literally forced out of his foot. We tried so hard with him, to be able to get him into a condition where he could play, but it was to no avail.

On October 22nd, 1977, we travelled to White Hart Lane to play Tottenham, who were seeking promotion back to the First Division at the first attempt. The previous week, the board had lamented the poor recent form and had remonstrated, 'Mr Manager, why can't we play with wingers?' I did, but I always played with one attacking winger and another that was withdrawn. But they kept on at me saying that they really liked wing play. Coming away from the meeting, I decided that I'd had enough. I thought, 'I'll bloody show you. I'll play with wingers.'

I looked at the next fixture. It was Tottenham away, who'd retained all their players from the previous year, and were a fluid passing team. They had Glenn Hoddle, Steve Perryman and John Pratt. They'd won six of their eight games, but had gone into this one on the back of a 4-1 defeat to Charlton so were desperate to return to winning ways. Knowing that they were favourites to win, and that other teams had been beaten when playing cautiously, I decided to go flat out on attack.

I thought that if we could get off to a good start by playing attacking football, and give ourselves something to defend, we might stand a chance. But I didn't count on Colin Lee getting four goals on his début. At 6-0 I looked down the bench to Gary Mabbutt, who I'd brought along to get experience of being with the first team as a fourteen-year-old, and asked him jokingly, 'How would you fancy going on now?' At that moment, a photographer popped up and caught me laughing. On Monday morning the newspaper read, 'How can Megson laugh when his team are getting beaten so badly?'

With about ten minutes to go, Glenn Hoddle made it 9-0. We

won a corner and Bobby Campbell jumped up and shouted to Stuart Taylor to push up. I told him sternly, 'Bobby, we're not going to get beaten by ten. Just sit yourself down.' Nobody had ever been beaten by ten goals on television and I wasn't going to be the first. The match ended 9-0.

We managed a draw and a win in our next two games, but then lost 5-1 away to Sunderland. I was at home after the result when the phone rang. It was Keith Williams from Portland Timbers. He asked if he could meet with me right away. I laughed. 'Well Portland is a long way from Bristol, Keith.'

'I've come for you Don. I'm in Bristol. Meet me at the Crest Hotel for breakfast tomorrow morning.'

I told Yvonne what had happened, and asked her if she'd like to go to America. 'Wherever you think is right for us,' was her reply.

The next day I walked to the Crest Hotel. It was little over a quarter of a mile from where we lived. Keith was there, and he offered me the chance to manage Portland and double my wages. Apart from the fact that I knew I was at the end of my tether, I knew that I loved America, and I'd love it for more than a week if I moved there. Given that I couldn't see any headway at Rovers at all, I decided to go down to the stadium and ask the chairman if I could make a split.

That night I went on TV to announce my resignation. I nearly broke down because I was genuinely upset. I'd spent seven years in Bristol and was leaving a lot of good people. A little tear came to my eye and Roger Malone, who was the interviewer, jumped on it but I just about held it in. 'Well, that's me done. I've enjoyed my time here.' I turned the television on that night and Roger Malone was talking to the chairman who was asked what he thought about me resigning.

'Well, it's goodbye Don Megson, hello Bobby Campbell.'

Well that said it all. It was as amicable a decision as you could get. I held my hand up. We were a bad side and Bobby did a good job to keep Rovers up. Without the lift from a new manager, I don't think Bristol would have stayed up that season.

A few weeks later Rovers played Bristol City and I took

Yvonne. As we walked through the park to Ashton Gate we passed some Rovers fans. The week before they'd been chanting my name. This time they sang, 'Megson's a wanker.'

I turned to Yvonne and said, 'That's football all over.'

14

City of Roses

A few weeks later I received another phone call from Keith. 'Don,' he told me, 'There's a league management meeting in New York next week. We'll go to it, and then you can come to Portland and have a look at videos of the team from last year. What do you say?'

I didn't really know how to respond. As a manager and player in England I'd always had everything done for me. If I was going anywhere on club business I'd be given my ticket, driven to the airport and given my passport. Keith, on the other hand, simply told me to report to New York. I guessed that it would be easy enough, so I bought my tickets and the next week caught the flight.

It had been a fairly mild winter in Britain, but I arrived at Kennedy Airport to find a foot of snow on the ground. Having only previously travelled there in the summer, I had no idea that they even had snow in America. I made my way through the airport lounge to the taxi rank. It was deserted. I mooched about until a taxi appeared out of the mist. It was a huge 4x4. A large Texan called it down, so I rushed over and asked him if I could go halves, then two other men joined us. I got out at the Plaza Hotel, right next to Central Park. It was a grand old building, one of the finest hotels I'd ever seen. At the time, Phil Woosnam was the League Commissioner, and the meeting was held each year. Being new to the league, a lot of the information went over my head, but it was a good chance to be introduced to the other coaches, and to learn a bit more about the draft process.

After the meeting, I travelled on to Portland. I spent a week being chauffeured around, getting a feel for the city, and watching videos of the previous year's performances. The 1977 season had not been a success for Portland. Under Brian Tiler, they had finished bottom of the Western Conference, a great disappointment considering that in their début season, they'd made it to the 1975 Soccer bowl against the Tampa Bay Rowdies. The team had been strengthened with Clyde Best and Stewart Scullion, two of the players from that Rowdies team, and both of them stayed with me, along with Willie Anderson, the former Aston Villa and Cardiff winger.

My one regret on taking over was that Brian's wife never spoke to me again in all the years that I knew her. She thought I'd stabbed Brian in the back and taken his job, but nothing could be further from the truth. I'd actually been Keith's second choice because he'd come over to sign up Jim Smith, the Blackburn manager.

The majority of the players were English, with some from the First Division but mostly from the lower leagues. I soon learned that for all the foreign players, the key to having a good NASL team was to have a core of skilful North American players. You had to have three on the field at any one time. Fortunately for me, Portland were already close to that. As I watched the videos, I'd occasionally turn to Keith to ask who the players were, and what their situation was. One player in particular, Ike McKay, impressed me, and Keith told me that Brian had been against bringing him back. 'How do we reach him," I asked.

Keith took a puff on his cigar, and laughed. 'If you want Ike Don, I'll get you to him.'

Ike was a teacher in Nanaimo, a small city around thirty-five miles from Vancouver, and it was a little remote. Keith chartered a seaplane to fly us up. I'll never forget landing on the lake when we arrived, splashing about on the water. We met up with Ike at his house and he signed straight away. His local school board initially refused to give him a leave of absence, but we got lucky.

My contract stated that I would live at home for three months a year to sign and scout players, and then bring them to Portland for the new season. Les Rigby was still with the club, and once I knew the type of players that I needed, we would meet up and he would match me to some suitable players that he'd seen. The first player he recommended was a defender, Clive Charles. He had come through at West Ham and was playing for Cardiff after a spell at Montreal Olympic. Clive became a coach for the United States national team after he retired, but sadly died of cancer at a young age. He loved my bones and always gave me everything that he had.

When I had lived in Bristol, I'd frequently watched Bristol City play. Their manager at the time was Alan Dicks, and he had two young players in the reserves, Brian McNeil and John Bain, who caught my eye on a number of occasions. I negotiated with Alan for the two of them to join me for the season, exactly the same as I had done with Graham Day. I took them for the season and City came to Portland for a friendly.

During their visit, we took City manager Alan Dicks and his assistant horse riding in Bend, a small town fifty miles outside Portland. It was Yvonne's forty-second birthday, so she also came, taking up a riding position behind the two. It was a dry day, and the trail was really dusty. The horses in front kicked up all the dirt and dust, which stuck to Yvonne. By the time she got to the end she was covered. She took it in good stride but was obviously unhappy.

I also started doing some of my own scouting work. My first game was against California Surf, and I wanted to check them out pre-season as a test to see what the standard of the league was like. My assistant Dave Givens and I flew down to San Francisco, and then drove out to Fresno to take in their game against the Oakland Stompers. In their line up was Mike Flater, a forward who'd played for the National and Olympic teams, and he impressed me enough to sign him.

After the match, Dave mentioned that the Vancouver Whitecaps were playing the following day, and that it would be good to take the opportunity to scout them as well while we had the chance. The distances between NASL clubs was so great that it was hard to keep tabs on the opposition. All was going well until it came time to return home when Dave realised that I didn't have my passport with me. You didn't need it for internal flights so I'd left it in Portland, and they hadn't asked to see it on the flight to Vancouver. This meant that I wouldn't be able to get back into the US.

Dave suggested that I should sit in the toilet until the plane was ready to go and then try and sneak on without showing my passport. That was a stupid idea, so instead we got his wife Nancy to go to my apartment, get my passport, and then fly up to meet us. When we told Keith what had happened, he failed to see the funny side. 'What the hell made you think of that, Dave? If he'd been caught he'd have been deported, and I'd have lost my coach before we'd even played a game.'

Alongside the Gant brothers, Bruce and Brian, I had my quota of Americans. The rest of the squad was split between older players coming to the end of their careers, and young players who hadn't lived up to their potential in the First Division. The majority of the older players came to America to squeeze another couple of seasons of first team football into their careers, and they took the experience seriously. As did some of the younger players who were there to prove themselves, and show their English clubs what they could do.

But there was always a minority who, with stars in their eyes and a desire to escape the dreariness of England, went off the rails. One of the first players Les turned me onto was a really good amateur player called Kelvin Norman, who happened to qualify as an American player through his parents. Les raved about him, so I agreed to give him a shot. Kelvin arrived a couple of weeks later, and Keith and I met him at the airport. We went through the standard procedure for new arrivals which was to get them off the plane, straight down to the office, then to the estate agents to find them an apartment, then to the furniture lease company, and finally to the car lot to get them a motor in Portland Timbers colours.

We left Kelvin at the car lot and set off back down to the freeway in Keith's Mercedes Sports. I loved that car. The speed limit was only fifty-five miles an hour and it was hard to keep the speed down because it was such a powerful machine. We were cruising along when Keith noticed a car coming down the slipway onto the freeway. It was in Timbers colours. ZOOM. It was Kelvin. Obviously he had no clue about driving in the States and the only test he'd had to pass was to drive 250 yards around the lot. Having told him to take his time and get a feel for the city and the roads, he'd got completely lost in the excitement. I turned to Keith. 'What a nutter!'

*****

Compared to the other stadiums in the league, the Civic Stadium was antiquated. There was no getting away from the fact that it was a baseball stadium which underwent some hasty modifications on match day. The worst problem was that the pitch wasn't flat and it had a drain in the middle which puddled when it rained. We took advantage of that fact, because we knew the best parts of the pitch to push the ball behind the defenders, and how far the ball would pull up in wet conditions. Another problem was that our pitch was made of Astroturf, which was experimental back then, and it started to show its age fast. Add all that to the fact that the pitches were a lot smaller than the ones in Europe, and that half of the pitches in the league had a baseball diamond made of sand in one corner, and you can understand that we sometimes struggled.

We lost the first game against California 1-0, and our early form was patchy. But by the time we played the Seattle Sounders on June 10th, 1978, we'd gone on a seven match winning streak, including a shoot-out win against the New York Cosmos. Both Portland and Seattle had established football fan bases, and it was the closest the league had to a 'local derby.' The game was dubbed 'The Rose Derby' because Portland was known as the Rose City – all the home fans were given roses before the kick off.

Yvonne was never the biggest football fan, but I remember she once got involved in an argument with a young Seattle fan at an away game over a John Bain penalty. The kid's parents got involved and they had a blazing row in the stands. Walking off the pitch at the end of the match, Neil told me, 'I'm not coming to a football game again with my mum.'

For that first match, the stadium was buzzing with excitement because we would equal the longest winning streak in NASL history if we won. We really battered them that night, with their full backs restricted to hitting us on the break, but somehow their goalkeeper, Tony Chursky, kept us out. There were fouls being given away everywhere, so in a way I was relieved when it got round to the shoot out.

The NASL had some interesting rules that set it apart from the rest of FIFA. The points system for example awarded six points for a win, and one extra point for each goal scored up to three per game. If the game ended in a draw it would go to extra time, and then after that, a shoot out. Players had to run from the thirty-five yard line and shoot within five seconds. Once you'd had a shot, it didn't make any difference what happened to the ball. If the goalkeeper managed to get a hand to the ball and it went up in the air and into the net, it would still count. A man with a horn would indicate when the time was up.

On this occasion, I was confident. We'd won all four previous shoot-outs that season, and I made sure that the players practiced before each match. But I didn't count on the referee Marjan Raus, a Yugoslavian who'd been brought in to raise the standard of refereeing in the league. Because Raus couldn't speak English, I'd been assigned an interpreter to help me communicate with him, who took his place beside me as the shoot-out began.

Seattle missed their first kick, but so did we. Les Parodi, an English defender, then put them ahead, so we were under pressure when Mike Flater stepped up. Mike charged towards Chursky, who dashed out and caught him on the heel just before he kicked the ball. The Seattle players thought that Chursky had got to the ball, meaning that Mike had kicked the ball illegally out of his hands, but Raus let the goal stand. Jimmy Gabriel, the ex-Everton midfielder and Seattle manager, rushed onto the field to confront Raus who beckoned for an interpreter to come and explain things.

Seattle missed their next two, but I was getting confused. A couple of times we'd managed to get our shot off, but the ball hadn't had a chance to cross the line before the whistle blew. I usually told the players to avoid blasting the ball as hard as they could but to find an angle, drop their shoulder, take the ball to their side and roll it into the net. But Clyde, instead of going flat out, pushed the ball forward, stopped, and then lobbed it over the goalkeeper. He got his shot off in time, but Raus blew his whistle as the ball bounced towards the net. Immediately, I grabbed hold of the interpreter and shouted, 'Go and tell him he doesn't know the rules.'

The interpreter spluttered that he couldn't, but I started to get angry, and yelled, 'GET ON THE PITCH!' Without thinking I grabbed him off the bench and pushed him onto the pitch. The crowd noticed, and started laughing. 'TELL HIM HE DOESN'T KNOW THE RULES!'

It turned out that Raus didn't know the rules. He thought that the ball had to be in the net within five seconds, not that the shot had to be hit within that time. Regardless, Seattle argued that Clyde had taken more than five seconds and the referee agreed. 1-1. The next Seattle player shot straight at our goalkeeper, Mick Poole, and the ball trickled across the line before he could save it. Again, it was ruled as taking too long. Our final shooter, Willie Anderson, drilled his shot into the upper right corner, and we won 2-1. Six days later we beat the New England Teamen to set a new league record.

The next game took us down to Florida to play the Tampa Bay Rowdies who had Rodney Marsh starring for them. Again, Raus was refereeing and he was on their side for the entire match. We lost 2-0, and after the final whistle Graham Day decided to tell Raus what he thought about his performance. Graham extended his hand as if to invite a handshake but then pulled it back as Raus reached out to shake it. Raus sent him off!

*****

Overall, my first season was a great success and only four losses in the last eight games stopped us from winning the Conference.

In the first round of the play-offs we beat the Washington Diplomats 2-1 in overtime, and then beat the Vancouver Whitecaps over two legs, 1-0 and 2-1. In many ways, Vancouver was as big a derby as Seattle, because of the number of Canadian internationals we had that were from the Vancouver area.

The only thing standing between us and the Soccer Bowl were the New York Cosmos. They were a massive operation, owned by Ahmet Ertegun of Atlantic Records. They had internationals in every position, including Franz Beckenbauer, Dennis Tueart, Giorgio Chinaglia, Carlos Alberto, and Werner Roth.

We should have come away with something from the first game, as I remember us having about twenty shots on target. After fifteen minutes, Brian Gant got the ball through to Stewart Scullion who managed to get the ball past their keeper but it was ruled out for offside. Two minutes later and the positions were reversed. Stewart got the ball to Brian and he headed in, but it was offside again. I went into the dressing room at half time thinking that we needed to contain them in the second half, perhaps nick a goal, and then the pressure would be on them.

Sixty seconds after the restart we were down. Dennis Tueart burst through our defence and popped one in. The score for the second leg was 1-0. The only chance we had of beating them was to play defensively. That's not to say that the Cosmos were invulnerable as they'd been beaten 9-2 by the Minnesota Kicks in the first of their Conference semi-finals.

I thought about what I'd do if I was playing against Beckenbauer. If I was told to stick with him and stop him playing, he wouldn't play. But if I joined the game for a second and drifted away from him, he'd get the ball and leave me behind. I needed someone who had the discipline to follow Beckenbauer wherever he went and nullify him from the game, enabling us to play ten against ten. The man for the job was Canadian, Peter Stanley. In pre-match training I told him to stay as close to Beckenbauer as he possibly could. 'Peter, you are his shadow and if he comes off the field and goes to the toilet, then you go with him and stand in the next stall.'

Beckenbauer soon got fed up of Peter and decided to swap

positions with Carlos Alberto. He went into the sweeper position while Carlos Alberto went up into midfield. Their hope was that Peter would start following Alberto, who was a full back, instead. I twigged this, and called Peter over to me. 'Peter, stay on Beckenbauer.' I knew that the German wouldn't have the discipline to stay at right back. When he realised what I'd done, Beckenbauer jogged over to me and gave me the tosser sign.

Though Giorgio Chinaglia put them ahead after half an hour, we were in the match right up until the last ten minutes or so when Dennis Tueart put away the second, but then the floodgates opened. Chinaglia, Beckenbauer and Seninho all scored within ten minutes. We lost 5-0. It was disappointing, but overall I couldn't have been happier with the season.

At the end of season debrief, Keith asked me what I wanted as a reward. I told him that I didn't want a bonus, and that I'd prefer to travel home to England on the QE2. Yvonne was with me, and together we arranged to meet Keith Eddy, an ex-Sheffield United player who'd played for the Cosmos, in New York. We walked round 5th Avenue and 42nd Street, and up the Rockefeller Building. When we got to the top, we looked over to the harbour, and noticed that the QE2 was missing. We found out that there had been a fault with the lifeboats, and that it was cheaper to repair the mechanism out at sea, rather than to pay the docking charges in New York harbour.

*****

The QE2 was superb. After meeting two ladies from Leeds on the first night, we made our way onto one of the three captains tables (the ship had three captains) This captain in particular was a Leeds United supporter, and took a shine to me, so we ate with him each night of the cruise.

On the second day, we visited the shopping arcade, and Yvonne fell in love with an Omega Seamaster watch. She decided that she wanted to buy it for Gary's birthday. I saw the price, it was £500, and told her we couldn't afford it. She only went and bought it without telling me and then tried to sneak it through customs. Unfortunately for her, information about every purchase over a certain amount was relayed to Southampton but Yvonne didn't know that.

When we arrived in England, we were taken to one side by the Customs officials and asked if we had anything to declare. I said no. So I was alarmed when they started opening our suitcases on the floor. They opened one case that was tightly packed, and an invisible dog lead that Yvonne had bought bounced out onto the floor. But they couldn't find the watch.

We were searched numerous times taking over an hour. Yvonne had hidden the watch in her underwear, and as they finished searching the first suitcase and moved onto the second, she hid it in the first one. We were then taken to the Customs office. There they told me, 'We know about the watch, Mr Megson.' I replied, 'What watch?'

It was then that Yvonne piped up in a coy accent. 'Yes. I bought a watch. My husband forbade me.' I had to do quite a bit of grovelling to make sure that the only thing we had to do was pay the duty. Thinking about it, I don't think Gary ever wore the watch more than a couple of times.

15

Lock Out

My second year in America was a damp squib compared to the first. Keith Williams stepped down as Chairman and was replaced by Don Pollock, a member of Keith's board. Don had good intentions but didn't have the money or the clout to do much good. In an effort to raise more money, he hired a man called Kent Cramer to act as General Manager. Kent was a typical handsome American giant who'd been a tight end football player for the Minnesota Vikings. He knew all the players for the Seattle Seahawks, and once took me round the club to view a training session. Their game preparation was first class and each position had their own trainer.

Previously, Keith Williams had done all the promotion himself, which had suited me because Keith and I got on. Given my previous experiences, I had a feeling my relationship with Kent wasn't going to be easy. I was very keen to be professional and get the players as close as I could to thinking about football, whereas Kent was more concerned with image. In America, the drive to succeed was very much about appearances as well as substance.

The first thing that he tried to do was to make the players stand to attention and sing the national anthem before the start of every match, just like he had done as a player. I knew that my British players wouldn't stand still for anything like that. Not only were they not brought up to respect flags, I knew they'd mess around during the anthem, maybe do a little jog or tell a sarcastic joke, simply because they viewed it as a distraction from the game. 'Look Kent.' I told him, 'The most important people in this club are the players. And if they don't want to do that, they won't, and it'll always be like that.'

Football was from Mars as far as most Americans were concerned, which made it all the more important that we advertised football generally and the club specifically. The local media had unlimited access to us, and I was on the radio and television almost every day talking about the team and what was going on, which was something that took a long time to come to the British game. I'd walk out of the main office in the morning and the media would rush over to me with cameras on their shoulders, microphones pushed into my face, asking me deep probing questions straight off at 9.00am.

Kent decided that we should spread the word about the wonderful game that was being played down at the Civic Stadium. He bought a crate of small banners that had 'Soccer Fever, Catch It' imprinted on one side, and the rules of football on the other. We were told to disperse the players around the city so that they could hand them out to people. I was told to walk around with two of the women from the office who Kent had asked to dress up as clowns. I personally thought it was disrespectful to have them handing out these while dressed up, but I didn't have much say in the matter.

Apart from that, there was the interaction with the fans. The club organised 'The Booster Club', which involved picnics and sports days, and the entire team and the coaching staff were mandated to attend, sometimes off the back of requests that were sent to the ground. Dr. Pepper sponsored us with drinks and equipment to run soccer tournaments in schools, which was more akin to babysitting than anything else. The ultimate aim was to get some of the American footballers, the six foot, three inch types, into soccer so they'd eventually filter into the NASL.

Keith Williams had told me that I'd find something very different with an American kid compared to a British kid. 'They're very focused on learning,' he told me and it was true. You could tell an American kid to practice kicking a ball with his left foot, and that you'd be back in three quarters of an hour, and he'd still be there doing the same exercise when you got back. Tell that to a British kid and inevitably he'd be juggling and messing about.

Mascots were another odd fixture and every team had one. The most famous of all was the San Diego Chicken Man, who earned a living as the mascot for all the sports teams in the city. The first time we played against the San Diego Sockers, they had a big cannon placed right behind the managers bench, and every time they scored they let a shot off. We had just levelled the scores when we won a corner. As Willie Anderson stepped up to take it, the Chicken Man ran in front of him and started strutting. Willie decided to play along. The Chicken Man moved back to the side of the pitch, and Willie stepped up again. The Chicken Man again moved onto the pitch. The crowd were loving it.

I wasn't. I got up off the bench and ran up the line to the corner flag. I grabbed hold of the Chicken Man's feathers, looked it in the eye and shouted, 'Ey, chicken. **** off.' The guy in the suit was really startled. Feeling proud with myself, I started walking back to the manager's bench. Then I realised that when I'd shouted at the Chicken Man, I'd been looking into the costumes eyes, rather than the mouth, where the guys eyes were. A few days later, I received a roll-up through the post. Inside was a poster of the chicken and it said, 'All the best for the season, Don.'

The next time we played in San Diego, one of our defenders hoofed the ball out of play when he was under pressure. The ball sailed out of bounds and nailed the Chicken Man right in his privates. He collapsed from the impact and all the players doubled over laughing. The game was being televised, and I remember the Sockers wanted to use the clip to make a commercial. I think for his own sake, it never happened.

Another memorable mascot was Krazy George, who performed for San Jose. George had a big drum and would walk onto the pitch at the beginning of games with a tiger on a leash. They'd walk so far before the tiger was put away, then a troupe of dancing girls would come on, while George ran up and down hitting his drum, encouraging both halves of the crowd to chant. All this on a playing surface that was too long and not in the best condition.

The origins of the Portland mascot were complicated. Jim Serrill was a local lumberjack who'd started attending Portland games with his family. One day he appeared at the gates with his chainsaw. The security woman initially refused to let him in. 'Are you crazy, you can't take that into the stands,' he was told. Jim was an old school kind of guy and stood his ground. Eventually, Keith Williams was summoned down to the gates, and he and Jim got involved in a big discussion about the traditions and culture of the region. Portland was a big logging city Jim stated, and therefore it was only right that lumberjacking be given the respect it deserved. Keith eventually let Jim into the stand on the condition he took the chain off his saw.

This happened a few times over the next couple of months, and Jim started to get more outlandish. He started dressing like a beaver with a great big tail. Then Keith came up with the idea of having a club tree that would be brought out at every home game. Every time we scored a goal, Jim would cut off a round and hand it to one of the fans in the stands. We even used to take the tree up to Seattle with us, hoping that we'd be able to cut off a piece there, but I don't think we ever scored when we did.

Jim was a character. Because he was a lumberjack he had all the tools, including a pair of irons that attached to his feet so he could dig into trees, and a sash that he could use to hitch himself up. One game, he noticed that two of the poles at the ground were connected by a cross member, so the next week he brought his climbing gear, scaled one of the poles and threw his rope over the top. He came down to about thirty or forty feet and started swinging back and forth on the cross member with his chainsaw turned on.

The act eventually became stale. During a particularly slow game, Keith convinced Jim to do some cheerleading. The crowd were pretty hostile, and quite a few gave him the finger.

Opposition fans were even less enamoured. We beat Vancouver at the Empire Stadium in the play-offs in front of 33,000 people. After the game, Jim started doing his thing and incited a riot. A group of angry fans came down from the stands to confront him, and one cold-cocked him with a bag of ice. Jim started defending himself with his chainsaw. The next thing I know, he was being escorted out of the country by the police.

Eventually, we had to let Jim go. Part of his act was that he'd bring his beaver tail through his legs and shake it about, pretending that it was something else. One time however, he made the mistake of going up behind a linesman and started humping him. The crowd started laughing, but the referee saw it and stopped it. Americans have a peculiar relationship with sex.

*****

Over the close season, I began the process of strengthening and rebuilding the team. Ike McKay decided against playing another year, and Mike Flater succumbed to a knee injury that kept him out for the entire season. All of a sudden, I'd lost the backbone of my American contingent. Other players such as Pat Howard, and Graham Day, had been on loan and I wasn't able to keep them.

I was at a loss over replacing Mike until Clive Charles put me onto Dale Mitchell, a Canadian who played for the Vancouver Whitecaps. Dale was a young striker, only twenty-one, and had asked his head coach, Tony Waiters, if he could have trials at other clubs to get more playing time. I contacted Tony and arranged for him that he'd come down to Portland for a trial. I knew immediately that he was a talented striker and signed him up later that week, sending him over to England to train with Stockport County for the close season. Being young, he was inconsistent. He'd go on a good run where he'd score plenty, then would go cold, but we persevered with him. He became a Canadian international and played at the 1986 World Cup.

Although we began the season with a 4-3 win over the San Jose Earthquakes, we lost the next three games and won only four of the opening twelve. One of my biggest problems was that the players went on strike the week before the third game, a home match against the Minnesota Kicks. Quite a few of the teams in the league had a beef with the NASL administration over wages and conditions. After a players meeting, all but three of my players, two of whom were Americans and not in the first team, went on strike. The ones that didn't were honest. 'This is my chance to play in the first team, I'm not striking.' The striking players stated that this was okay and wouldn't constitute 'scab' behaviour.

One of the players who wanted to play was reserve goalkeeper Jim Gorsek, who was a bit of a lone ranger. I never saw him socialise with the rest of the team and I wondered at times whether he actually slept in the stands. He didn't have a car, but somehow was always early for training, and would stay late to practice his kicking. On my way home, I'd see him at the bus stop, sitting in the gutter, waiting for one of only a handful of buses that went by each day. My first choice goalkeeper, Mick Poole who'd played for Rochdale for many years, was in awe of him.

There was only one option apart from cancelling the game. 'Right,' I announced to Kent. 'I'm going to hold open trials on Monday. Get the television station over here.' I held a press conference. 'This coming Monday, Portland Timbers will be holding open trials,' I stated. 'Anyone who has the desire to play for the Timbers, report to the Civic Stadium at 10:00am for a trial.'

On Monday morning, I drove down to the stadium as usual. As I turned the corner, I noticed a quarter of a mile queue stretching down the block. They'd come from everywhere just to have a kick. I got my coaches together and we decided to play a series of games lasting a quarter of an hour each way. I stood at the front and said, 'Okay guys, we're going to hold a series of trial matches. Whatever position you think you play in, just go and stand in it.'

As the games were played, I walked round inspecting the players. 'No chance. No chance. No chance. Mmm, he can play a bit. The others, thanks but no thanks. Next lot!' This went on all day, and I eventually whittled them down to two teams. 'Okay guys. Thanks a lot. Out of those who can, who is going to come tomorrow morning?'

The next day, the two teams played against each other a few times, and as the day wore on I formed a forward line from the two teams that I thought looked best, and did the same with the defence. I had them play against each other. As I went on I discarded a few more players, until finally I had a team I was happy with. One of the players was a teacher, and he was so good I offered him a professional contract, but he turned down the offer because he was on good money at the school he was working at. All those who didn't make it were given free tickets to the game.

I always thought of myself as a good motivator, and in the dressing room before the match, I worked magic. I got the players that wound up with my 'We will fight them on the beaches, we will never surrender, don't ask what your country can do for you' spiel that they could hardly see straight. 'This could be your chance to become a Timbers player permanently. And if it doesn't work out that way, you will always be able to say that you played for Portland Timbers at the Civic Stadium with pride.' I sent them out ready for battle.

One of the players that night was Scott Meiggs. He couldn't get any higher, even if I'd given him drugs. At one point, Jim Gorsek kicked a ball deep into the Minnesota half and it bounced in the direction of their goalkeeper who rushed out. As he was about to catch it, Scott came in with a rugby charge that knocked him about six yards into the net. 'You've got to calm down a little bit,' I told him at half time. 'You'll be sent off if you play like that.'

In the end we only got beaten 2-0, which wasn't bad for a week's work. I'd approached the task just like I was coaching the first team, and made them think they had a chance. What really annoyed me was that only two of the Minnesota players had gone on strike. The next day, someone told me that ninety per cent of the players in the league had broken the strike and played. In a way, I was pleased that my players had stuck together and shown a little bit of solidarity in refusing to play. If all the players in the league had done the same, they might have got what they wanted.

Things were getting a little desperate by the date of the Rose Derby on June 9th, 1979. I was completely focused on getting the team back to winning ways, and it didn't help that I had a falling out with Kent. He wanted me to drop the players off a mile away from the stadium with bunches of roses, and ask each of them to converge on the stadium. They were to walk down each aisle of the stands handing out roses to the fans. Finally, they'd come onto the pitch and wave to the crowd. Bluntly, I told him that he had his priorities wrong, and refused to do it. We won the game 2-0 with goals from Clyde Best and David Butler, a striker who I had taken from Seattle.

Although we won our next two games against the Edmonton Drillers and the Toronto Blizzard, we then went on a six game losing streak, which pretty much ended our hopes of the play-offs. Kent was spooked, and announced that if we lost our next game against the Atlanta Chiefs, every fan would receive a free ticket to the game against Fort Lauderdale. For a team that was struggling to find money, it seemed ridiculous to hand out 11,000 tickets at a loss. Immediately after the Atlanta game, which we lost, Kent sacked the Public Relations Director John Hahn who accused Kent of trying to 'force feed' the media with stories in an attempt to increase attendances.

I was also having problems in the dressing room. Stewart Scullion in particular left me disappointed. Stewart was a good player who had been in the game a long time, but he'd indicated to the media that he wanted to move on to a new club. I didn't want to let him go, but for whatever reason, he just wouldn't entertain Jimmy Conway, and eventually they clashed. Stewart knew someone who played for another team, and during a game, Jimmy overheard Stewart ask him, 'See if you can break Jimmy's leg.'

Jimmy wasn't the kind of person to get into a fight, but obviously he could take care of himself, and as soon as the two entered the dressing room at half time he went for Stewart. Thinking that Jimmy was trying to cause an incident, I intervened shouting, 'Get out of it!' As soon as I found out the truth, I knew that Stewart's time at the club was up. I was upset at having to do it because I thought he was a good man. He cried in front of me, telling me that it wouldn't happen again, but I didn't really have a choice. For some unknown reason, and I never got to the bottom of it, he and Jimmy just loathed one another.

*****

With three games left, we flew to Philadelphia to play the Fury, with still an outside chance of getting into the play-offs. I was quietly optimistic but it was obviously misplaced, because we got beaten 5-0. At full time I felt terrible, and was walking across the pitch aimlessly in my Timbers tracksuit. Suddenly, a girl walked up to me and threw her arms around my neck. 'Great party last night,' she whispered. By the time I could react, she'd already gone.

Jimmy Conway was at the side of me, and as I turned to him, he gave me a consternated look. 'Boss,' he said. 'They let you down last night.' Jimmy took his game very seriously, and it quickly dawned on me that what he meant was the players had spent the previous night out partying late. A fly on the wall in the dressing room would have lost his hearing. I cut the legs off the lot of them.

There were distractions everywhere, and not just in the night life. We were once down in San Jose for an away game, and as each player ran onto the pitch, they looked to their left. After the last player jogged on, I walked forward to look, and there were twenty absolutely gorgeous girls wearing tassels. I thought to myself, 'How the hell do I compete with that?' After the match, we walked around the back of the stadium where a group of old fashioned railway carriages painted in San Jose colours were parked up and partied into the late hours.

I often had to keep the players confined to the hotel, such was their energy for the lifestyle. American women threw themselves at anything that had a British accent. Elson Seall, a player who would have jumped off a bridge for me, used to worship striker Clyde Best. We were once in a hotel in the Deep South, I think it was Houston. Elson was getting restless and repeatedly asked Clyde if they were going to go out on the town. Clyde told Elson in his slow drawl that they were going nowhere. 'Elson, we don't know where the local black guys aren't allowed to go.'

16

Signing a Superstar

In August 1979, Don Pollock announced that the Timbers had to find new investment if they were to remain viable. The team was owned by Oregon Soccer Inc. a company made up of about fifty investors, including Don and Keith Williams. The price for not having reached the play-offs was a $500,000 loss. Phil Woosnam, the Commissioner of the NASL, was invited for crisis talks and Dave Givens, my assistant, and John Leas, one of the trainers, were laid off.

I tried to carry on with the job of management. Another year meant another renewal of my American contingent, and I wasn't sure where to find them. I knew that the US national team were due to play in Bermuda in early October, four days before the annual league meeting in Florida, so I decided to fly out two days early, meet up with Phil Woosnam, and watch the match with him. Though the United States won, the game was a disappointment because none of the best players played, but I decided to go for the right back Glenn Myernick, who was nicknamed Mooch.

I then flew to Florida. I was three days early, so I decided to relax, sunbathe, and hang around the bars. Being October, it wasn't particularly sunny so I thought I'd be fine in the sun. There on the beach, watching the motorboats zoom around the bay, I felt great. That evening, I walked into a restaurant and the waitress walked up to me saying, 'You've caught some rays today, honey.' I saw my reflection in the glass and I was a bloody beetroot red.

The meeting was a waste of time. Most of the agenda was devoted to looking over video clips of draft picks, and I'd already completed all my American transfers. The next day, I went out with Dennis Viollet, the former Manchester United forward, who was Assistant Manager at the New England Teamen. He took us to a downtown café. We entered, and walked through another door which led to a spiral staircase. At the top was a bar, with red leather seating. 'Sit yourself down there,' Dennis said.

I ordered a Jack Daniels. We'd been sat for a while chatting, when suddenly a door opened and four girls entered. They were wearing flimsy bikini bottoms, and nothing on top. One of them started dancing in front of me and then put her foot up on my shoulder. Dennis turned to me and said, 'If you don't tell her to get down, it'll cost you a hundred dollars.'

'WOAH!' I shouted. 'Just happy with my whiskey thanks!'

We went out again the next night and caught a glimpse of the other side of American life. We went to a nightclub and sat in a corner booth with our drinks. There was a guy sat with a girl not far from us, and at one point he got up and walked to the rest room. Another man took his place, but when the first returned, the two started arguing. One of the men took out a gun. 'DENNIS!' I shouted. 'Come on, we're off!

*****

While I was in Florida, the Timbers were sold to Louisiana Pacific, one of the biggest logging companies in America. Unlike Keith Williams and Don Pollock, who'd been well off but hadn't had the money to throw at the club, Louisiana Pacific were big hitters. But they treated the Timbers in the same way they'd treat one of their lumber yards, which was as an asset to make money. The President, Harry Merlo, was a typical American sports franchise owner in that he had a reasonable knowledge of American sports but knew nothing about football. He wanted to micro-manage everything, and was very hard to satisfy. It proved almost impossible to educate him about the game.

Replacing Kent Cramer as General Manager was Peter Warner, who had been a missionary in Jamaica before settling in Oregon in the late 1960s as a pastor. Because he was British and a bit of a talker, the Americans had taken it as gospel that he knew a lot about football, and he'd previously fulfilled the role of Oregon Soccer Commissioner as well as being a NASL referee performance evaluator. His role under Merlo was not easy. The league regulations were almost impossible to follow, and he had to have a weekly budget sheet on Merlo's desk by 6.00am every Monday morning. He also had to present the weekly strategy for dealing with the press, who Merlo perceived as 'our enemies.'

I parted ways with Dennis and flew home to England for the winter. It was always good to catch up with friends in Bristol and have the chance to scout players. It was also an opportunity to catch up with Gary, whose career was starting to go places. Since I'd taken over at Portland, he'd broken into the Plymouth team. Malcolm Allison, one of his previous managers, thought that Gary had a good mind for starting attacks and spotting killer passes. 'He has the makings of a fine sweeper, Don,' he told me. I agreed, except that in my mind, Gary would have to be an offensively minded sweeper, because he wasn't the most physical of players, and not that great at heading the ball.

By 1979, Malcolm had been replaced by Bobby Saxton who was more interested in the transfer fee he could get for Gary than his career. I was helping Gary to train at Eastville to keep his fitness up when Everton came in for him, but for a while it was uncertain that the transfer would happen because Bobby and Everton manager, Gordon Lee, were playing games with each other over the transfer fee. Gary wasn't interested in the fee. He just wanted the opportunity to play in the First Division.

Louisiana Pacific had given me a lot of money with which to build up the club, and I fully intended to get the best players I could find. Looking back however, I think I made a few mistakes. I talked to Les Rigby, who told me that Manchester City were trying to trim their squad and had a few players available. I went to see their assistant manager Tony Book about their centre half Tommy Booth, but he wasn't available. I talked to Jimmy Conway, who had played for Manchester City, and he recommended Willie Donachie, a midfielder, and Stuart Lee, a big striker. I initially told Tony that I was interested in both of them, and we agreed a fee, but I quickly cooled on Stuart. I attempted to renegotiate the deal but ended up having to take him.

Another player who underwhelmed was John Pratt who came with a big pedigree from Tottenham where he'd played hundreds of games. I made the cardinal sin of buying John on a blind recommendation, the only time I ever did so. At the back of my mind was a memory of him scoring a fantastic goal on *Match of the Day*. Based on that, I assumed that he wouldn't be a duffer, especially when he turned down a contract extension at Tottenham to join us. But he wasn't the player I'd thought he was. Likewise with Gary Collier, a defender who had starred for Bristol City during the years I'd been managing Rovers but had failed to impress after a move to Coventry City.

Before returning to the States I went to see Les Olive, the secretary of Manchester United, to see if United had any players I could take on loan. Les had been at the club for many years and had even played in a couple of games as a goalkeeper before the war. He told me that the club didn't have anyone for me, but during our conversation it emerged that the team were going to Hawaii for their pre-season. Remembering Bristol City's trip to Portland, I suggested that they make a pit stop and play a testimonial game against us. The manager, Dave Sexton, agreed to it, so out they came. They didn't send the strongest squad, but Martin Buchan and Lou Macari played, and we matched them in front of a good crowd. We'd persuaded Harry Merlo to give free tickets for the match to our season ticket holders.

One of the biggest problems I had with the new owners was their desire to sign a 'superstar' for the team. Since the New York Cosmos signed Pele in 1974, every team had clamoured for a marquee signing. Tampa Bay had Rodney Marsh, San Jose had George Best, New York had Franz Beckenbauer, and Seattle had Bobby Moore. And just before the start of the season, Peter and Harry decided it was time for Portland to join in. At that time, there weren't that many superstars around who were willing to come to America. But Peter had an idea. He owned a poster of Rob Rensenbrink, the Dutch winger, wearing the Holland strip, and that became his focus. 'We can get him,' he told me.

Knowing that Peter was serious, I decided to do some homework. Is he playing? Is he still as good as when I saw him for Holland? Is he even fit? The answer to all three questions was no. He'd just had a cartilage operation a couple of weeks before. I told Peter expressly, 'No. I don't want him. He's not going to be able to play for half of the season.' I considered the matter closed, but a few days later I came into the office early, and walked in on Peter having a meeting with Dennis Roach, one of the first real modern football agents. Peter looked up as I walked across the room: 'I've got Rob for you Don. He's flying over tomorrow.'

The following day we went to the airport. As he walked down the steps and onto the tarmac with his family I noticed that he was limping, and had a brace on his knee. We shook hands and then he gave his plane ticket to Peter without saying a word. He'd upgraded himself into First Class, and given Warner the regular ticket to pay for. I could tell that he wasn't going to be happy dinking around in small hotels because he was class all the way through, and used to playing at the highest level.

On the way back to the stadium, I asked Rob if he'd be able to do some ball juggling to make the media happy. He was announced as the superstar who was going to set Portland alight with his magic left foot. He started doing some tricks with the ball and looked impressive, but I was wincing every time he turned, half expecting him to fall to the ground in pain. The next day I sent him to a rehabilitation clinic.

The season started poorly with four losses in five games. I'd spent over a $1 million on Gary Collier, Willie Donachie and Stuart Lee, and $1.2 million more on Rensenbrink, but the team wasn't working well together. Rob was so far ahead in terms of footballing ability and skill that the other players often couldn't keep up with him, and the fans quickly grew tired of watching stray passes when Rob attempted a move that the rest of the team couldn't read. After a disappointing loss to Tampa Bay Rowdies, the media also started to turn on me. A journalist barged up to me with a microphone, and without introducing himself, demanded to know why we were a bad team. I had to be on my guard. 'We are not a bad team,' I said. 'We just had a bad night and a bad result.'

The only game in which we came close to playing to our full potential was a 4-2 away victory against the Washington Diplomats. All the talk before the match was about Rob getting up to form and putting one over Johan Cruyff, who was in the Washington line up. Rob and Dale Mitchell both got a brace.

We lost the next game against Minnesota, but subsequent victories made me think that we'd turned the corner. But after a loss to the California Surf, things came to a head. We'd flown to Florida for a game against Fort Lauderdale, and were in the hotel when I got a phone call from Peter. He told me that he'd been in a conference with Harry, and was flying down the next day to talk to me. I asked him to meet me by the hotel pool, but Peter insisted on meeting me in his room. Without telling me that I was sacked, he told me that Merlo wanted him to take over as manager. He was obviously embarrassed to be telling me that he was taking my job, so I tried to put him at ease. 'Don't worry. I'm up to here with it to be honest. As soon as I get back to Portland and get paid up front, I'll be out of your hair.'

I told the team, and then went up to my room and packed my things. I overheard the players having a meeting in the room below. It crossed my mind that they might rebel against the decision, but then I heard John Pratt say, 'Okay, we've got make the best of a bad job here. We don't need to do anything that he says, but we've got to play the game that the gaffer has set up and we'll take it from there.'

Instead of going straight home, I headed to Miami with Les Rigby, who was with us for a few weeks to discuss players. If I'd gone straight home there would have been reporters waiting for me. I flew back a few days later, once the story had gone cold, and walked off the plane into an empty terminal.

*****

I'll never be able to adequately describe how much I loved America. From the first time I visited with Wednesday, I'd always wanted to live the American lifestyle, but Yvonne never settled. Though she made friends, and enjoyed the tennis club she joined, it never took the place of England. She didn't mope about, but you could tell she missed Bristol. I don't know if I'd have taken another job in America, because then my marriage would have been under threat.

To an extent I was sympathetic. We'd enjoyed living in Bristol a lot, and the social life had been brilliant. But Portland had been absolutely perfect for me. I'd come over to England for three to four months, hire myself a nice car, go to all the games, and see all the people that I knew in the game. I'd go to Manchester with Yvonne to see the rest of the family, and having spent time away, we'd get on famously.

Things were complicated by the fact that I'd bought a house immediately after taking the job. It had originally belonged to my bank manager, who had planned to move in until his wife fell in love with Honolulu on a trip to Hawaii and refused to leave. I mentioned to Keith Williams that I needed to furnish the house, and he put me onto a friend of his that wanted to sell some high quality furniture. I walked into his flat and did a double take as the furnishings were immaculate. I bought it all for $4,000, the beds, sideboards, everything.

The first time Yvonne came over to Portland, I picked her up from the airport, and as we drove over the hill to the house I said, 'What do you think of that. It's yours. I bought it for us.' She loved the house, but as time went on, and she didn't settle, it became a stressful place to be. When her mother died in 1979, she decided to move back to England permanently. And after I left Portland, I wasn't able to get a Green Card, meaning I couldn't look for another job in football, so I had no option but to sell the house and follow her back.

Before leaving, Yvonne had told me that there was next to no work going in Britain for young people, so we decided that Neil would stay behind in Portland. He was seventeen going on eighteen, had gained a bit of the American confidence, and relished the opportunity to stay. He wasn't cocky, but he'd been bred to stand out and speak up for himself, which was the American way. He made speeches at his graduation, something I don't think he'd have had the nerve to do if he'd stayed in Bristol.

We decided to get Neil enrolled at a college, the University of Puget Sound, and arranged for him to stay with a family that we knew in Portland. If I'd stayed in America, he probably would have stuck at it, but with both me and Yvonne in Britain there was a buffer, and he soon decided that he wasn't learning anything. He phoned me and said that he was moving to Dallas with a friend to work on the oil rigs. I told him that he was going to stay in school and considered the matter closed. But a couple of weeks later he phoned again, from Dallas, and told me that they couldn't find any work. A that time, cable television was just starting to become popular, so they ended up getting jobs selling cable door to door. The network eventually made its way to Portland, so they moved back and started doing the same job there.

Neil also carved out a football career of his own. Whilst still at school he'd played for Lake Oswego High School, and then after he returned to Portland, at a pitch complex called Delta Park. The Argentinean, German and Scandinavian immigrants used to play there, and eventually formed a league. It was while he was playing in that league that Freddie Goodwin, the ex-Manchester United player and Seattle Sounders coach, spotted him. He took him to Seattle where he played with Joe Corrigan and Ricky Villa in their final NASL season.

From 1983 to 1992 Neil played indoor football for the Tacoma Stars, where he was coached by former Arsenal player Bob McNab, and later on by Leicester's Keith Weller. Of the three footballers in the family, he is the only one to have been capped at international level. In 1988 he made appearances for the United States in two World Cup qualifiers against Chile. He still reminds Gary and me that he is the only international player in the family.

17

Blowing Smoke

My first reaction upon returning to England was to regret that I'd left in the first place. I'd not been all that young when I went to Portland, and it had cost me a lot of traction on the English scene. My name was lost among a slew of younger managers and players, an important factor in lower league football. As hard as I tried, I just couldn't get a break, and for the first time in twenty five years, I reverted to joinery work.

I was doubly unfortunate in that I came back having sold my house in Bristol, and that meant I had to live with Gary in Liverpool while I looked for another job. I had my American furniture shipped over, but because Gary had his own furniture, he put mine into storage. Unfortunately, the storage place burnt down and I lost all my possessions, including a grandmother clock that my dad had won in a sprinting competition at Blackpool in the 1940s.

The next summer, Gary moved to Sheffield Wednesday, and after helping him sell his house in Liverpool, I moved back to Sheffield with Yvonne. In an effort to stay in touch with the game, I started going to watch Rotherham United. It was there I met up with Brian Tiler again. He'd returned to Britain, and had hooked up with Anton Johnson, the owner of Rotherham. Anton was the fifth generation owner of Johnson Butchers, and had bought the club on a whim when he heard they were for sale on *Match of the Day*. He'd made quite a few enemies in the game because of his supposed reputation for ducking and diving, but my time with him was largely positive.

Anton knew through Brian that I was out of the game. The three of us started to meet up regularly at the Carlton Club in Rotherham, and over drinks one night, Anton told me that he wanted to sell and buy another club. I carried on watching Rotherham, in the hope that I would be foremost in Anton's mind if he needed to hire a manager. Likewise, Brian was fishing for a Director of Football position.

The first club we went to see was Wigan Athletic. At the time, Wigan were controlled by Freddie Pye, who'd spent a lifetime in football, and later became Chairman and President of Manchester City. The three of us walked into the Boardroom, and were greeted by Bobby Charlton, who was a director of the club, as well as caretaker manager. I'd not seen Bobby since we both stopped playing. We had a good catch up, but nothing materialised in terms of taking over the club.

Then we went to Bournemouth. They'd just sacked David Webb, and put Harry Redknapp in as caretaker manager, but things weren't going well – they'd just been beaten 9-0 by Lincoln. We met with Harold Walker, who was a gentleman of the game, and Anton agreed to buy the club. Both Harry and Ivan Golak were pushing for the job, but I ended up getting it.

The first thing I needed to do was to get an Assistant Manager. I got talking to the Chief Scout, John Kirk, who was affectionately known as 'Captain Kirk' and he recommended I keep Harry Redknapp in the role. 'Harry knows his stuff,' he told me. I told Anton that I trusted John's judgement and that I'd give Harry a chance to prove himself.

After winning my first two games in charge, Anton and I sat down to discuss what needed to happen to improve the team. It turned out that we had very separate goals. I wanted to get the club going by signing good players so we could push for promotion the next season. Anton wanted to focus on maximising the clubs profitability.

The terms of my working relationship with Brian was confused. As Managing Director, he was responsible for the running of the club on a day to day basis, while I was responsible for coaching the team. However, just before the press conference that announced Anton's takeover, Brian told me that I was to tell the reporters that Anton had backing from a group of American investors, and that money would be available to spend on the first team. 'Don, It'll sound better coming from you than me.' I knew it was an outright lie, but I went out and said it anyway. 'There's going to be backing from America,' I stated. 'No the details don't concern me, I just know that money will be available.'

The previous year, the club had signed Charlie George on a short term contract to try and boost home attendances. He hadn't worked out but Anton and I decided it might be worth another shot. There was only one person who fit the bill in my mind, and that was George Best. George was largely retired, and had been playing as a guest for a couple of teams in Hong Kong, but his registration was still held by the San Jose Earthquakes in the NASL. Brian contacted Milan Mandaric, who owned the club, and was told that George was surplus to requirements. I didn't really get involved in the negotiations but I don't think George cost us any more than $7,000.

The club arranged a meeting with George at the Churchill Hotel in London. I told him that I wanted him to play six home games to boost the gate, and in return, would give him his international clearance, allowing him to play for any club in the world.

All the managers George ever had couldn't handle him, so I wasn't even going to try. There were no restrictions. If he was there on Thursday, he'd train Friday and play on the Saturday. And in spite of his bad knee, he did everything I asked of him. On Friday morning in the cold, he trained harder than I ever anticipated, and stayed behind to get himself in the best possible shape. During the television interview before his first game, against Newport County, I told him jokingly, 'If you don't know what to do George, put it in the net.' We lost the game but George did okay, and we doubled the gate.

At the time, Brian and I had not yet found places to live, and were staying in a hotel that the club used regularly, and on the weekends that George came down to play, he stayed with us.

Being around George, I started I realise the pressure George must have felt throughout his playing career. One night we were playing pool and a woman walked in saying, 'Which one of you is George Best?' At the time, George had a huge beard so didn't look like the George of old. He stood forward and said, 'I'm George.'

'Well I don't want to meet you,' she said, 'but my husband thinks I should.' All George could do was smile. There were no airs and graces about him at all. He was a genuinely nice man and everyone liked him.

Each season, Bournemouth organised an open day for school kids up and down the country to come to the club and take part in training sessions. That year there must have been around twenty-five teams playing, and we decided that each team would have a Bournemouth player to coach them. Naturally, all the kids wanted to play with George. It would have been unfair for him to play with just one team, but George offered to play with them all. He put on a different coloured jersey, and played three to five minutes with each team. It might have been just a few passes, but that was enough for each kid to be able to say that they'd played with George Best.

As the kids were leaving, Brian, George and me were stood at the side of the main training pitch. I was holding a size four ball, the smallest you could get. George piped up, 'A tenner if I can land that ball on the cross bar.' Brian was game and said that he'd have a piece of that, and I joined in as well.

George placed the ball down and pushed it on without a care in the world. Ping! Straight on the cross bar. He told us that he'd put the money on the 2:30pm the next day and that if he won, he'd give us our money back. There was little chance of that happening.

Most of the time, George would bring Mary Stävin, winner of the Miss World Contest, with him to games. But on the Thursday before his second game, I was in the lobby of the hotel and he walked in with Angela, his wife. He'd been drinking, and when she'd found out that he wasn't going to get to Bournemouth by himself, she'd pushed George into a taxi because otherwise, he would have walked out of his house in Southend and gone straight to the pub. She dropped him off, got in the taxi back to the train station, and went home.

As it turned out, we had problems sticking to the six home games agreement. George's third game was actually an away match, against Southend. George wanted his son Callum to be able to see him play, and I agreed, not thinking that George would count the match as one of his games. He played, and counted it. And, after the game against Lincoln, I got a call from Bob Martin at Bradford City who asked if George could play for us at Bradford. I told him that George didn't need to play, and to ask George. Bob personally offered to pay him £1,000 if he played, and George agreed. I told Brian that I'd go to Bradford with the players, and that he was responsible for picking up George from London on the Saturday.

Not long after I'd got to Bradford however, I got a call from Brian who said that George hadn't turned up. I told him to see if he could get a hold of Mary as she knew his usual haunts. An hour passed, and Brian rang me back. They'd found George in a closed nightclub with his wife Angela. Mary ran out crying and Brian followed. A minute later, George followed telling Brian that he wanted to calm Mary down and that he'd be back in a minute.

I cut in, 'You didn't let him go did you?'

George had done a runner. The Bradford chairman was not happy because they'd sent out posters and fliers advertising his appearance. The gate went up regardless though. It was the only time George let the club down, but I wasn't fussed because he'd arranged it with Bradford and not me.

George actually ended up playing only five league games for us. I'd signed a striker called Ian Thompson from Salisbury, and part of the deal was that we'd play a game against them. We agreed to let George play in the game and their gate rocketed. He hardly touched the ball in the first half because the other players weren't giving it to him. At half time, I decided to send on Harry Redknapp, and told him to pass the ball to George every time he could. Harry showed his class as a player by giving George the ball ninety-five per cent of the time. George counted the friendly as another game, so after the last match of the season against Wigan, the club gave him his international clearance. I can't say how highly I rated George, and how much I enjoyed his time at the club.

*****

My first three months at Bournemouth were fantastic. We went from the relegation places to mid-table security. We made money on the George deal, and money appeared to be flowing a little more easily. Brian and Anton decided that the team deserved a holiday, so we took the players to Porta De Luz for a week. I was getting on really well with Anton and Brian at this point, and pre-season training went well. But overnight, things soured. At the start of pre-season I re-stated the need to make signings. They gave me free reign to sell any of the players that I didn't want, and re-assured me that we could start fresh.

The first problem came with the sale of Nigel Spackman to Chelsea. They'd been interested in him for a long while and, as far as I was concerned, we'd put the phone down on £125,000. A few days later however, Alex Stock, who was Bournemouth's chief scout knocked on my office door. 'Don, I thought that was really bad money for Nigel.' He'd been told that we'd sold Nigel for £25,000.'

The next sale was John Impey, who went to Torquay. He'd played over two hundred games for Bournemouth but had developed a bad back. Towards the end of the season we had to take another centre half as back-up in case his back went into spasm. He was disappointed to leave, and made it very clear when he blanked me during a pre-season friendly.

Later in the summer I took Yvonne to Kassiopi in Greece. I kept in touch with Brian while we finalised the Ian Thompson transfer. One day, he rang with news: 'I've got him for you.' Brilliant, I thought. That's Thompson ticked off. Then Brian told me we'd paid £42,000 for him. My heart sank like a stone. Ian was a non-league player, and that was a heavy fee. 'Well that's market forces Don,' said Brian. 'That's how much he cost.'

I'd let six players go by then and only replaced one. I returned from Kassiopi and resumed the search for players. Harry was an expert at finding players, that was his strength, so I asked Brian how much money we had to spend. It turned out that all the money had gone on Thompson and I'd have to make do with free transfers. From that moment on things got desperate. Harry and I went to West Ham and spotted three players that we liked the look of, but Harry knew that the West Ham manager, John Lyle, wanted £25,000 for the cheapest. It was futile even trying to bother. I started the season with Thompson, John Beck, and a squad full of inexperienced players.

We lost the first seven games. I was smoking cigars at the time and was sat on the line during one game when a Bournemouth fan shouted, 'Megson, Megson, Megson. Stop sitting there smoking your cigar and do something.' I looked down the subs bench and saw apprentices staring back at me. There was nothing I could do.

Our goalkeeping situation was farcical. Our first choice keeper was Ian Leigh, a reasonable prospect, but because of the financial situation Brian decided that we didn't have to carry two goalkeepers. 'I can get you one the next day, if we need him.' The first game of the season, Ian broke his thumb. Brian rang around, and managed to bring in Neil Ramsbottom, a veteran who'd been good but was now in his mid-thirties.

My favourite kind of goalkeeper was tall and good at kicking, and Neil was neither of those. Often his kicks wouldn't even make it to the forward players, and would land on the heads of the opposition on the halfway line. I had to get one of our defenders to take the goal kicks which put us at a disadvantage, because then he was in the six-yard box rather than on the half way line.

My relationship with Brian quickly deteriorated. He was a great personality and we had good laughs. When we were going in the same direction he was great. He'd been brought into the American way of thinking, that the General Manager took care of everything off the pitch, while the manager looked after the team, but he started interfering in nearly everything that I did.

The number of practice balls we had, the number of towels, everything was under scrutiny. Brian had the drive to get where he wanted to be, even if it was at the detriment of someone else. Eventually, I decided to move my desk to another part of the stadium rather than share an office with him.

Anton never put me under any pressure even though we weren't winning, because the gates weren't going down. But one day Brian walked in without notice, told me that he'd been on the phone with Anton, and that I was sacked. I was shocked, but in some ways relieved. 'Brian, we're not getting on and I'm not happy. No problem with that from me. As long as I get paid, I'll get out of your hair.' I went to the players and told them that I wouldn't be with them the next week. John Beck told me, 'I'm absolutely gutted for you. You had your hands tied behind your back.' Then I called a press conference and told everyone that I was leaving.

About an hour later the phone rang. It was Anton. He was in London attempting to buy Fulham Football Club, and told both of us to get down there right way. Brian offered to take me down in his car, but I was that angry that I drove down separately. Anton was waiting for us. 'I pay you to make money,' he told Brian, 'not to sack managers.' Then he said that I was going back into the club tomorrow. I told him that I couldn't do that and I wanted out as it would take someone with more motivation to lift the team.

A few days later, I spoke with Anton, and he asked me who I thought was best for the job. I knew that Brian had earmarked someone from up north, but I recommended Harry, just as John Kirk had recommended Harry to me. Even back then, he knew the game. 'As long as you make sure that Brian doesn't control everything that he does, you'll be okay.'

I didn't leave Bournemouth immediately. I stayed on as scout until the end of the season so I could get paid. In the meantime, Anton moved his attention to Southend United. One weekend, he invited me to spend the weekend at his house in Grays. He told me he was thinking of sacking Peter Morris, the manager, and suggested that I could take over. We travelled to Roots Hall, and walked into the supporters bar. Sitting at the bar was Bobby Moore. We started talking and I found out that he'd virtually been promised the Southend job. I knew I didn't want the job, but it must have been awkward. Peter was still manager, and in walks another manager with the owner. Bobby must have heard alarm bells ringing in his head.

*****

The next year, my father died at the age of seventy-eight. He'd had diabetes for years and had moved into a home because of his poor eyesight. At the time, insulin was administered with a huge syringe, and he'd started to get his dose wrong. He'd either give himself too much or not enough, and was forever going into comas. If he came to visit, we'd always have to check on him. At least in the home he got the right medication.

I continued to do joinery work, whilst trying half-heartedly to get back into the game. My calf injury had continued to dog me over the years, and by the time I took the Bournemouth job, I was in agony after each training session, and became increasingly reliant on Harry to do the physical work. I used to go running and the muscle in my leg would tighten up after fifteen minutes. There wasn't a cat in hell's chance of me getting back into the game the way I wanted because it was all pain, and I couldn't face having to hobble back to my car every time I trained.

I did get a couple of interviews though. The one I came closest too, and was a little bit disappointed over, was the Chesterfield job. It came up in 1988 and I got an interview.

I'd got to know Paul Hart who'd played with Gary at Wednesday, and I thought he'd make a good coach, so I intended to suggest him as my assistant. I met the board and for my mind gave a really good interview. Afterwards, the chairman told me, 'Well Don, you've put us in a little bit of a situation. We were very pleased with your interview but we'd not really thought about getting an experienced manager. We had thought of getting somebody who is new to the job, to take us along with him.' Turns out they'd already interviewed the person they wanted – Paul Hart.

Epilogue

A Life in Football

I enjoyed my life in football as much as anybody would. I don't think there's a soul in the world who'd say no to the opportunity of playing football professionally, and if you told me I could have the time again, I wouldn't hesitate in saying yes.

Accomplishment in sport is final, you win or lose. But character is unique to experience. I worked hard through my career to be the best player that I could be. The fact that I'm most proud of is that I played for five managers at Sheffield Wednesday, and played forty-two games in a season under all of them except Danny Williams. Anyone of them could have looked at me on the training pitch and thought, 'He's not what I need.' But they didn't, and in all I made close to 450 appearances for Wednesday, and another thirty or so for Bristol.

Looking at my career as a whole, I hesitate to say it, but I was a nearly man. I played with the England defence, was called up to the shadow squad even, but I never got an England cap. I never won the league, but came as close as you can by finishing second to Tottenham, who had the highest number of points in a generation. I reached the FA Cup Final, but didn't win it. I was never relegated, but I came close.

I grew into a competent coach, a motivator who worked well in the good times. In my own way, I influenced a few men to take their game on to the next level. I got all the razzmatazz of promotion from the Third Division, I went over to America, managed against the New York Cosmos, and nearly got to the

Soccer Bowl. I maintain that I could have turned Bournemouth around if given the time. After leaving Bournemouth, I tried like mad to get back into football, and its fair to say that my retirement from the game was enforced, but I don't have any regrets.

The other winner was my family. I miss my brother Cyril, but I still keep in contact with my older brother Derek. After giving up the weightlifting, he focused on his career as a plumber, and eventually made his way up to Council Inspector. He still calls Manchester home. Cyril played many years in the Cheshire League, which was a very high standard league with a lot of ex-pros. He played hundreds of games for Hyde and Stalybridge Celtic, and was one of the outstanding players on the local scene.

I couldn't have picked a better partner than Yvonne. Being with her was never a chore, and we did loads of things together. At the same time, we were always happy to go off and do our own things. Yvonne, for example, wanted to come home from America, but with Neil over there, it was less than a year before she decided to go and visit him. While she was there, Neil offered to drive a car down from Portland to Los Angeles for a friend, and Yvonne decided to join him. On the way, she got to thinking that she could fly directly from LA to Australia, so she took $7,000 out of my USA bank account and flew to Australia for a month to visit her sister. That's just the way our relationship was.

I couldn't have asked for better sons. They chose different paths, but both of them have achieved success in life. In 1994 when the Seattle Sounders reformed, Neil joined and helped them win the USL League play-offs in 1995 and 1996, making over a hundred appearances. He then managed the team for four years from 1996 to 2000 and has coached various teams in Washington State since then. He has now settled in Tacoma and is Director of Coaching at the Harbor Soccer Club in Gig Harbor, Washington. I still visit once a year, and still love the American way of life.

I've got two grandsons, and both showed potential to make it as professional players. I always wanted Gary's son Simon to play in a Wednesday shirt at Hillsborough. While Gary was manager at Nottingham Forest, Simon trained with them, and also had a month at Hillsborough to see whether he was good enough.

He did well and had some potential, but when a player doesn't stand out, they get the dreaded conversation, 'Well you did okay, but you're no better than what we've already got.' Sometimes its about giving the right look, or a certain coach taking a shine to the way that you play on a certain day. Unfortunately, it never happened for Simon, who is now making his way in finance.

Neil's son Alex has decent potential, and has bugged me over the years to bring him over to England to see if he can get a trial, being very confident that he could make it here. He's made himself into quite a star in the National Indoor Soccer League playing for the Chicago Riot, the Syracuse Silver Knights, and Missouri Comets.

I was with Yvonne for fifty-two years before she succumbed to cancer. From the moment I met her, my life blossomed. She was my soul partner. There was nothing about her that I didn't like. She wasn't a wallflower, and I don't think that would have been right for me. She wanted to be involved in everything that I did.

From the moment the Doctor informed her of the illness, her reaction was to simply state, 'I've got cancer and there's nothing I can do about it. I'm just going to get on with my life.' She didn't want to see the pity in people's eyes, so didn't tell anyone apart from me right up until the end. When asked if she wanted a McMillan nurse she said, 'No, I've got my Don.'

*****

It was a proud day for all of us when Gary was appointed Wednesday manager. He was a Wednesday fan growing up and had taken the club to his heart in two spells at Hillsborough under Howard Wilkinson. He also spent time at Nottingham Forest, Newcastle and Manchester City. At Norwich, his final posting of note, he showed off the wealth of experience that he'd gained, and they called him 'The General.'

I'd watched occasional games for Gary throughout his managerial career, from Blackpool through to West Brom and Leicester, and was always available to give him advice. I'd often spend the day fitting a kitchen, and then I'd go and watch a game under Gary's direction and give my opinion on the players that were being watched by his scouts.

Gary is a very good motivator and a good manager. He knows what he wants to do and how to do it. An achilles heel for both of us might be that we don't respond well to interference, and like to be in charge of a teams destiny. Gary once told me, 'Opinions are just opinions. I have to make decisions, and they have consequences.' When you are very driven to do well, it is bound to have an effect on how you approach the job, simply because all criticisms come to the manager, and you have to feel that it is solely your responsibility for the performance. It's very difficult when interference from other quarters plays a part in your decisions.

Every manager has his ups and downs, but Gary has had his fair amount of success. I think his most notable team was West Brom when he took them up, and kept them up. He also did well at Stoke, and also at Bolton. He liked Bolton, liked the club, and had a good relationship with the Chairman regarding transfers, but the fans never took a shine to him. It would always have been hard for him to follow Sam Allardyce, and Sammy Lee had already failed to do it before him. The only place where it didn't really happen for Gary was at Nottingham Forest, where he had a good relationship with the Chairman, but player power played a large part in upsetting the harmony of the dressing room.

Gary and I have similar ways of thinking about football. We both like attractive football, but recognise that you need a certain level of ability among your players to be able to adopt a style of play pleasing of the eye, and that won't be detrimental to the team's success in terms of results. You can only play a type of football that suits the players that you have, and its the wrong approach to try and make a team play a style of football that isn't suited to them. If you try it, you're not being the type of manager that furthers a club, and you're asking for trouble.

You can't advocate playing just short passes, in the same way you can't advocate just playing long passes. A pass can only considered successful if its completed, and the difference is that the percentage of achieving success with a long ball is lower than with a short ball. A lot of it has to do with the playing conditions. In England in the 1960s, even Old Trafford, after two months of the season, would have a pitch that had no grass on it. In those conditions, short passing was so much harder than it is now, and it was much safer and more effective to be direct and get the ball up the field with one pass.

The first time I walked through the Wednesday players' entrance after Gary was made manager, it was like going back sixty years. I could have been blindfolded, and I'd still recognise the smell of the place. The dressing room was still exactly the same as it was the day I left the club in 1970. In my mind's eye I could see my shirt hanging on the Number Three peg.

I went to most of the home games during Gary's tenure. I'd have lunch in the boardroom, and then watch the game from the Executive Box as a guest of Milan Mandaric. I'd catch up with old colleagues I'd not seen for years. Then afterwards I'd go down to the reception room for visiting managers and trainers and chat with Gary about how the game had gone.

Anything that football might have lost in terms of soul is probably made up for by the sheer spectacle of it now. The facilities, the pitches, the comfort, the music, everything about the match day experience is better. I remember playing First Division football against Northampton Town in 1960 on a muddy cricket pitch, with the supporters on one side of the pitch carrying their own chairs, as there was no stand. It has lost a bit of that raw excitement I think, but it's not my place to preach. It's not seen as the just the working man's game anymore.

Wednesday are definitely a big club. You only have to look at the history and how they achieved things over the years, but it has gone through some hard times. It's really fallen behind compared to the Premiership clubs, and Hillsborough looks a little worn down. But as long as the club survives, and continues to provide a positive experience, then it will have succeeded at the most important thing, which is to be there for its fans.

I still keep in touch with many of the team from my days. Gerry Young still lives in Sheffield, Peter Swan lives in Chesterfield, while Alan Finney lives in Doncaster. Derek Wilkinson still lives in the Manchester area, and Wilf Smith lives in Nuneaton.

For many years, I also visited John Fantham, who also lived in Sheffield. It was a sad day for all of us when he passed away.

One of the best times I remember when the old players got together was the occasion of Stanley Matthews' eightieth birthday celebration. In fact, there were quite a few of them around the country, and we were invited to the Sheffield one. As each man arrived in the reception room before the meal, Stanley was there to greet him, with John Charles standing beside him. I was one of the first to arrive, and shook Stanley's hand. 'Hello Don. Good to see you. Hope you're well.'

I was quite impressed that Stanley knew who I was. And as more players arrived he'd shake their hand too. Ron Springett, would arrive. 'Hello Ron good to see you.' It turned out that as each person walked through the door, John was whispering into Stan's ear. 'Johnny Quinn. Gerry Young.' Still, it was a great occasion, all the former players in one room, reminiscing about the great times we'd had together. Even Stan had a few stories, though he did fall asleep during dinner.

Bristol Rovers are still a great club with a real sense of community and friendship, and I'm still honoured to have taken them through one of their greatest spells. I've gone down a couple of times, most recently to take part in the club's 125th anniversary celebration. Present were many of the former managers and a couple of players who lived in the Bristol area. I also went down for the fortieth anniversary of the Watney Cup win. Peter Aitkin, who still works at the club as Community Manager, walked up to me. 'Hello Boss,' he said. It was like nothing had changed.

It proved to me that I really was lucky to have experienced a life in football, to have the opportunity to make people happy by doing the thing I was most passionate about in life. It hit home how much I've enjoyed doing this book, and reliving all the great experiences I got out of the game. To the fans, and the players, to Sheffield Wednesday, Bristol Rovers, Portland Timbers and Bournemouth, and all of my family, I simply say, thanks for the memories.

Chris Olewicz is a history graduate, writer and researcher from Sheffield. He currently works in welfare services, and watches Sheffield Wednesday as often as he can. This is his second book, following *20 Legends: Sheffield Wednesday*, a book he co-wrote with Tom Whitworth.